# The Wedding Planner

**The Wedding Planner**

First published in 2017 by 256
2nd Floor, The Mill
Greenmount Avenue
Harold's Cross
Dublin 12
Ireland
256media.ie

© Confetti

ISBN: 978 0 99 576771 3

Written by Laura Cunningham

Art Direction by Tanya Ross, *elementice.ie*

Illustrated by Carol Mahon, *carolmahon.com*

Contributions from Aimée Moriarty,
Aoife Valentine and Aisling Keenan

Author photography by Lili Forberg
Hair and makeup by Róisín Malone

Printed and bound in Poland by Opolgraf, *opolgraf.com*

This book is typeset in Brandon text 11pt.

For Jackie

# Contents

# Welcome To The Wedding Planner

There are many things that become a much bigger part of your life when you're engaged. Initially, you might feel like you drink more Prosecco than water, with a constant excuse to celebrate in your arsenal. You'll soon know things about flowers you never knew you needed to know, and obtain an encyclopaedic knowledge of cake fillings – things could be worse. The presence of other people's opinions also multiplies at a rate of knots. Realising this early on and practicing a selection of neutral responses like, "Thanks - I'll keep it in mind..." should see you right.

Confetti has been Ireland's favourite wedding magazine for more than 16 years now, so you could say we know a thing or two about planning one. We've seen trends come and go and watched weddings grow and change, to become the wonderfully creative celebrations they are today. Our best advice is to plan how your wedding will feel, and not just how it will look. When the day comes and you're saying those magic words together, the shade of your peonies or height of your macaron tower won't matter a damn. (Nor will that relative's opinion about your guest list, by the way.) It'll all melt away, leaving only love. A wise lad once told us that it's all we need, and we reckon he knew what he was on about.

In this book, we aim to guide you through the finer details and help you plan a day that's truly you, without stressing yourself out too much. Sure, it's a huge day in your lives, but it's meant to be a bit of craic too. If you take one thing away from this book, let it be that your wedding is just that - yours. It can take whatever shape you want it to; simple or flamboyant, large or small. In fact, if you decide to ignore everything we've written and get married on a Monday morning in yoga pants, that's fine too.

Whatever you do, enjoy every second. And when it's all over, try not to be too glum. After all, weddings are all about beginnings. Not only will you get some nice gifts, you'll also bag a bestie for life – not bad going, eh?

*Let's do this!*

# Getting started

## WED-IATORS, READY!

# Okay...Go!

You're engaged! ... Now what? When your ring selfie has clocked up 500 likes on Instagram and you're almost fed up of Prosecco (almost), settling down to actually plan your wedding can be a daunting task. But, like any big job, it's a whole heap less scary when it's broken down into smaller parts. Our nifty and extensive 12-month planning guide will do just that and, suddenly, with each small task assigned a mini-deadline, that overwhelming to-do list will seem totally achievable. You've got this!

Just like our mammies taught us, if you start with the hard bits, the rest will be a doddle. With that in mind, we're tackling the tough stuff in this chapter. Our handy guides will ensure that budgeting doesn't totally wreck your head and that carrying out the boring legal bits will actually be quite lovely. Yay! And remember, you're not alone. Now's the time to choose your wedding A-Team. Your bridesmaids and groomsmen are in this with you and will relish being part of your adventure – so choose wisely and don't be afraid to lean on them.

Hindsight is 20/20 and learning about the most popular planning mistakes will help you avoid them yourself. We're also shining a light on pesky hidden wedding costs, so you don't get caught out.

Before any of this kicks off, it's important to take some time to sit down together and discuss what you both want this wedding to be. Determine your priorities – do you want a large or intimate wedding? What parts mean the most to you? Share your wildest dreams and chat about the things you've always wished for from your wedding. After that, it's time to knuckle down...

## Happy planning!

# YOUR 12-MONTH
## Planning Timeline

### 12 MONTHS TO GO:
◇ Set your budget
◇ Decide on a number of guests
◇ Compile a guest list and start gathering addresses
◇ Book a reception venue and ceremony location
◇ Book a celebrant
◇ Pop the question to your bridesmaids and groomsmen

### 11 MONTHS TO GO:
◇ Book your band, photographer and videographer
◇ Research potential suppliers for flowers, cake, décor, hair and makeup etc.
◇ Start your wedding dress research

### 8-10 MONTHS TO GO:
◇ Shop for and order your wedding dress
◇ Order stationery
◇ Book a florist
◇ Order your wedding cake

### 6-7 MONTHS TO GO:
◇ Send Save The Dates
◇ Secure transport
◇ Plan and book your honeymoon
◇ Hire a hair stylist and makeup artist and book your trials

### 4-5 MONTHS TO GO:
◇ Shop for bridesmaids' dresses
◇ Organise the legalities – book an appointment and give at least three months' notice to registrar or priest/religious celebrant
◇ Arrange travel vaccinations and check passports/visas
◇ Attend pre-marriage counselling, if required (Catholic ceremonies)

### 2-3 MONTHS TO GO:
◇ Shop for groom's and groomsmen's suits
◇ Shop for bridal accessories
◇ Create a gift list
◇ Send invitations
◇ Order your wedding rings
◇ Attend dress fittings and hair/makeup trials
◇ Choose your music for the ceremony and reception

# 1 MONTH TO GO:

◇ Prepare your ceremony with your officiant
◇ Have your final wedding dress fitting
◇ Finalise your Order of Ceremony and booklets
◇ Follow up any unreturned RSVPs and finalise guest numbers
◇ Write up a seating plan
◇ Send out as many final payments as you can
◇ Write vows
◇ Decide who will do readings and toasts
◇ Create a day-of schedule and send to vendors

# 2 WEEKS TO GO:

◇ Give venue or caterer your final guest count
◇ Break in your wedding shoes
◇ Pick up dress, groom's suit and rings

## WEEK OF:

◇ Confirm vendor delivery and arrival times
◇ Finalise transportation arrangements for ceremony and reception
◇ Final waxing, eyebrows, manicure appointments
◇ Organise cash to be paid to suppliers on the day
◇ Pack overnight bag

## DAY BEFORE:

◇ Dress the venue – make sure you have lots of help!
◇ Provide all wedding suppliers with a contact for the day
◇ Hold ceremony rehearsal and optional rehearsal dinner
◇ Get a good night's sleep!

## YOUR WEDDING DAY!

◇ Give wedding bands and any remaining vendor payments to your best man or maid of honour
◇ Give gifts for parents to best man or maid of honour for after the speeches
◇ Drink water and eat
◇ Enjoy every second!

**Create your own detailed schedule in our planner on page 217!**

# THE LEGAL BIT

There are a million and one things to plan when you're getting married, but they'll all be pretty useless to you if you haven't got the legal requirements sorted. In order for your marriage to be valid, there are three conditions to satisfy...

You must have the capacity to get married. You have to be aged 18 or over (or under 18, with permission of the Circuit Family Court or High Court), you must not already be married or in a civil partnership, and not be closely related.

You must consent to the marriage. Certain individuals with intellectual disabilities or mental illness are not legally able to consent in Ireland.

You must give three months' notice of your intention to marry, in person, by appointment, with your local registrar. You both must be available to attend. You'll need...

◇ Both of your passports, PPS numbers and birth certificates, and divorce decrees or death certificates of your previous spouse, if necessary.

◇ If either of you are not Irish citizens, you need an Apostille stamp from the relevant embassy on your birth certificate (everywhere except Denmark, Italy, France, Belgium, Estonia, Romania and Latvia), and evidence of immigration status. You may also be asked to provide a Letter of Freedom to Marry to confirm your civil status from your home country. If any of your documents aren't in English or Irish, you'll need a certified English translation.

You'll inform the registrar whether you will have a civil, secular or a religious ceremony; the intended date and location; details of your proposed solemniser; and the names and dates of birth of your two witnesses. This should be submitted on a form downloaded from the HSE website (*hse.ie*). You will pay the €200 notification fee and sign a declaration that there's no lawful reason why you can't get married.

If there are no legal impediments, they will issue your Marriage Registration Form, which is the authorisation to go ahead. Bring this form on your wedding day, as you'll both be signing it, along with your solemniser. It should then be returned to the registrar's office within 30 days. Following that, your marriage will be legally registered. You can then purchase a marriage certificate from any Civil Registration Office for €20.

# Oh No You Didn't!
## 8 WEDDING PLANNING MISTAKES TO AVOID

**Mistake 1: Looking at venues before you've settled on your numbers**
This can waste time and lead to disappointment. Draw up your guest list, work out your budget and then make a list of venues that work for both, before you set foot in one.

**Mistake 2: Spending a single cent before you've drawn up a budget**
Set an overall amount and then decide how much you're willing to allocate to each element. You may regret purchasing sundry items early on, when you then have to scrimp on or skip something more important to you down the line.

**Mistake 3: Trying to do it all yourself**
Wedding planning is no mean feat. If you take on too much, you may end up sucking the joy out of the whole process for yourself, so don't be afraid to ask for help.

**Mistake 4: Giving yourself too many jobs on the day**
Dress the venue the day before and assign a point person to field questions, answer your phone and deal with any mishaps or problems that may occur on the day itself.

**Mistake 5: Hiring 'friendors' instead of vendors**
Trust us, your brother's wife's best mate's cousin is NOT the best choice of photographer. Hire the best people you can afford and ignore any pressure to do otherwise.

**Mistake 6: Not loving your 'plan B'**
If you choose your venue for its awesome outdoor ceremony space, make sure you're really happy with its indoor option too. You don't want your plan B to feel like a disappointing compromise on the day, if the weather doesn't play ball.

**Mistake 7: Not hiring a videographer**
It's the one thing we hear most from recently married Irish couples. If you can afford a videographer, get one! *More about this on page 91.*

**Mistake 8: Too much downtime between ceremony and reception**
Wedding days can be the wrong kind of long if your chosen church is a massive trek from your venue, or there are endless hours before dinner. Keep things tight or lay on some daytime entertainment.

*Just say yes,*
*JUST SAY THERE'S*
*NOTHING HOLDING*
*YOU BACK*

Snow Patrol

# SETTING A BUDGET

When it comes to planning a wedding, setting your budget is probably one of the least romantic, but most important, parts. Working out how much you want to spend, can afford to spend, and where exactly that money is going to come from is a challenge, so it's one worth getting on top of from the beginning.

Most Irish couples pay for their weddings themselves, through savings, or a loan, or both. While the tradition of parents paying has fallen by the wayside, many still contribute in some way. If your, or your partner's, parents are happy to help, chat to them early on about what they'd like to contribute. If you're uncomfortable talking about cash, perhaps see if they'll pay for something specific such as your dress or flowers, or pick up the tab for the catering or transport.

Once you've established a number, look at where you'll get the money. Will you save a certain amount of your salary each month, or perhaps approach your bank or credit union? It's best to be very realistic early on, as this avoids racking up high interest credit card bills later to pay any difference you hadn't expected. Starting married life off in unexpected debt is not something anyone wants, so be realistic when figuring out what you can afford to save and/or borrow.

It's important to sit down, without any pressure of what you 'should' be spending on each part of your wedding, and decide as a couple what's most important to you. Pick two or three things you don't mind spending more on, and some you're happy to scale back on, if needs be. You might find you're really keen to have the best photographer around and you're happy to opt for a more budget-friendly gown to accommodate it. Let your priorities guide your budget.

Take a look at the results of our wedding survey on the next page to see what the average spend for most Irish couples in each area of planning is. Of course, costs will vary widely depending where and when your wedding is, and what exactly you're looking for, but it's handy to know the average when initially setting your budget so you don't vastly underestimate or overestimate your costs. It's not uncommon to be initially shocked at just how much everything wedding-related costs. In fact, it's a rite of passage for every newly engaged couple.

Wedding bills rack up fast, so it's always worth including a contingency amount of around 5% of your total budget, as a just-in-case fund.

# Average Wedding Costs 2019

Every year, Confetti magazine carries out the ultimate wedding survey, to guide future couples and establish the average costs of organising a wedding in Ireland.

### Engagement

◇ The average spend on an engagement ring in Ireland is €4,055.

◇ The most popular months to get engaged are December (18%) and February (11%).

◇ The average length of an engagement in Ireland is 19 months.

◇ 12% of Irish couples become engaged at Christmas time. Just 2% of Confetti readers get engaged on Valentine's Day.

◇ In male/female couples, 98% of grooms ask their bride to marry them.

### Planning

◇ The average overall wedding budget in 2019 is €28,614. It was €27,120 in 2018.

◇ 46% of couples pay for their own wedding, while 38% get financial help from one or both sets of parents. A lucky 4% of couples' parents foot the bill.

◇ Savings cover the cost for 34% of Irish couples.

◇ 37% go over budget.

◇ The average spend on a wedding photographer is €1,890.

◇ 75% of couples hire a videographer and the average spend is €1,357.

◇ On average, Irish couples spend €398 on wedding transport.

### Hen/Stag

◇ Irish people pay an average of €240 to go to stag or hen party.

◇ For 49%, the hen/stag party takes place in another city or country to their own.

◇ The average number of bridesmaids and groomsmen in an Irish wedding is three apiece.

## Venue

◇ Irish couples spend an average of €12,754 on their reception venue.
◇ A hotel venue is first choice for 41% of couples, while 24% opt for a country house setting.
◇ At 54% of Irish weddings, speeches happen before the meal.
◇ Average ceremony costs (celebrant/church fees) are €467.
◇ Church weddings are on the decline, with 51% of couples marrying at their venue/elsewhere.
◇ 36% of Irish couples ban phones/cameras at their ceremonies.

## Fashion

◇ The average spend on a wedding dress is €1,909.
◇ The average spend on wedding shoes and accessories is €368.
◇ Grooms spend an average of €366 on their suit.
◇ Couples spend an average of €195 each on suits for their groomsmen.
◇ The average spend on bridesmaids' attire is €160 each.

## Beauty

◇ Couples spend an average of €345 on a makeup artist and €335 on a hair stylist.

## Entertainment averages

◇ Wedding band       €2,164
◇ Ceremony music     €495
◇ DJ                 €325

## Details

◇ 9% of people surveyed hire a wedding stylist (up from 5% in 2018) costing an average of €964.
◇ 48% of couples forgo favours.

◇ The average cost of wedding flowers is €650.
◇ Wedding cake       €414
◇ Stationery         €410
◇ DIY décor items    €599

## Wedding guests

◇ The average number of guests at an Irish wedding is 145.
◇ For a single wedding guest, 70% say they give €100 as a cash gift. 20% give a generous €150.
◇ 72% of couples say they give €200 as a cash gift between them.

## Extras

◇ 74% of couples don't take out wedding insurance.
◇ The average amount spent on a honeymoon is €5,864.
◇ 61% of Irish brides change their names – less than 1% of grooms change theirs.
◇ 65% of recently married couples said they didn't make love on the night of their wedding.
◇ 69% of soon-to-be-married couples say they aren't bothered about making love on the night.
◇ 96% were living together before they got married.
◇ 12% already have children together and 7% have children from previous relationships.
◇ Just 2% have been married before.
◇ The average age of a bride or groom in Ireland is 31.

# HIDDEN WEDDING COSTS

Don't get caught out with unexpected expense. Remember to budget for these sneaky little items - it all adds up!

### A taxing matter
When requesting quotes, make sure to ask whether the price is inclusive of VAT. That extra percentage could really dent your budget.

### Night-before accommodation
Venue fees will often include accommodation for the night of your wedding, but what if you'd like to wake up there on the morning of your wedding? For a private venue, this might be a big expense.

### Beauty budgeting
You've booked the best makeup artist and hair stylist you can afford, but remember that trials cost extra, and you might feel the need to have some additional treatments for your hair and skin in the weeks approaching the wedding. Many brides also like to buy up a whole new product stash before their wedding, and that'll cost a pretty penny.

### Wedding week wardrobe
Even if you're not having a rehearsal dinner and day-after shindig, you're going to want to look your best in the days around your wedding, so rooting something old out of the wardrobe isn't going to cut it. Having a 'day before' and 'morning after' outfit will take a lot of stress away, so make sure to account for this.

### Under armour
Buying the dress of your dreams is not where your bridal budget ends, remember to account for accessories, shoes, a veil and, the most-often forgotten part, shapewear. *See our complete checklist on page 60.*

### Cake cutting
This is often included in the package, but it's worth checking if your venue charges for cutting and serving your wedding cake, as it can cost up to €200.

### Feeding the team
Remember that you'll need to feed your photographer, videographer and wedding planner and include your band and DJ in the numbers for evening nibbles.

### Paying for postage
An often-forgotten cost, postage can be pretty pricey, so factor it in when budgeting for your wedding invitations and Save The Dates.

### Visas and vaccinations
If you're heading off somewhere exotic on honeymoon, don't forget to calculate the costs of the various injections and visas that you may need for certain destinations when writing up your budget.

# BUDGET WORKSHEET

| ITEM | QUOTE | PAID | BALANCE |
|---|---|---|---|
| **FASHION/BEAUTY** | | | |
| Wedding rings | | | |
| Dress/Alteration | | | |
| Veil/Accessories | | | |
| Hair/Makeup | | | |
| Suit | | | |
| Groomsmen's outfits | | | |
| Bridesmaids' outfits | | | |
| | | | |
| **DÉCOR** | | | |
| Flowers | | | |
| Stationery | | | |
| Centrepieces | | | |
| Draping/Lighting | | | |
| Favours | | | |
| | | | |
| **RECEPTION** | | | |
| Venue hire | | | |
| Wedding meal | | | |
| Arrival canapés | | | |
| Arrival drinks | | | |
| Wine/Prosecco | | | |
| Evening finger food | | | |
| Wedding cake | | | |
| | | | |
| **CEREMONY** | | | |
| Ceremony venue/Celebrant | | | |
| Ceremony music | | | |
| Ceremony décor | | | |
| | | | |
| **VISUALS** | | | |
| Photography | | | |
| Videography | | | |
| | | | |
| **ENTERTAINMENT** | | | |
| Reception music | | | |
| Band | | | |
| DJ | | | |
| Other | | | |
| | | | |
| **MISCELLANEOUS** | | | |
| Transport | | | |
| Hen/Stag | | | |
| Insurance | | | |
| Bridal party gifts | | | |
| Spouse gifts | | | |
| Honeymoon | | | |
| **TOTAL:** | | | |
| **BUDGET:** | | | |
| **OVER/UNDER:** | | | |

# The 10 Budget Commandments

**Thou shalt prioritise**
We can rarely have everything, so decide what really matters. Big foodies? Stretch to that venue with the amazing menu and don't bother with favours. Music lovers? Get the best band you can afford and ditch something less important.

**Thou shalt be realistic**
Your heart says black-tie ball for 500 in a stately home, but your bank account says bridal BBQ in your folks' back garden. Remember that this is about marriage, so don't completely overstretch yourself for the sake of one day. Some of the best parties don't cost the earth.

**Thou shalt not covet thy neighbour's wedding**
Just because your mate dropped €500 on some designer shoes doesn't mean you have to. Personally, we'd prefer to invite five more guests!

**Thou shalt embrace thy spreadsheet**
Buying 'bits' without counting the cost is the number one way of going over budget. Even if it's just matching socks for the groomsmen, write it down. You're less likely to spend mindlessly if you're holding yourself accountable.

**Thou shalt honour thy father and thy mother**
If they're helping to pay for your big day, they've earned a couple of tables of pals, at least. Keep that in mind when you're booking your venue and budget accordingly.

**Thou shalt remember the Sabbath day**
Planning gets old quickly if you don't give it a rest. Have a 'wed-min free' weekend once a month.

**Thou shalt not fill**
Give serious thought to the amount of 'plus ones' you hand out and don't feel under pressure to invite your whole office. Just make sure the ones you love are there.

**Thou shalt not take the name of thy credit union in vain**
Keep your bank or credit union on side and your account in the black. You might need them when you're hit with an unforeseen expense.

**Thou shalt bear honest witness to thy skillset**
If you're not exactly crafty, what makes you think you'll suddenly enjoy creating 1,000 tiny, folded, paper cranes? Spoiler alert: You won't. And the materials will probably cost as much as buying them from Etsy.

**Thou shalt chill thy beans**
The temptation to go crazy in the last few weeks buying 'finishing touches' can be all-consuming. Know when to draw the line.

# DO I NEED A WEDDING PLANNER?

## DIY or SOS? This should give you your answer...

No longer reserved for the super-rich and US brides, wedding planners are becoming a much more mainstream matrimonial choice here in Ireland. The benefits are obvious; someone else does the legwork while you choose flower shades and show up for menu tastings. And, let's face it, handing over responsibility on the day to someone you know has everything under control is the dream. But do you really need a wedding planner, or is that peak notions? Let's talk...

### How busy are you?
If you have the time to dedicate full weekend days and the odd evening to planning, you might relish the challenge, but if you're both working full time, have kids and can't answer your phone during business hours, chances are wedding planning will take its toll.

### Do you like event organisation?
If you're a natural party planner, you'll probably take it all in your stride and enjoy every minute. If the thoughts of throwing a big bash brings you out in a cold sweat, consider getting some help.

### Have your wedding party got you covered?
If your maid of honour is quite involved and your groomsmen are always up for a challenge, chances are that, between the lot of you, you've got this.

### Are you a fussy pants?
Be honest with yourself – will it irritate you if something's not perfect? If your venue's coordinator is a detail ninja, she's probably on top of things. If not, you could consider hiring a day-of coordinator.

### Are you getting married abroad?
It's very advisable to hire a planner, if yours is an international affair. They're your man on the ground, they know all the best vendors and can make sure you're not being ripped off by anyone.

### Is yours a DIY affair?
Converting your parents' barn into a party palace, or erecting a marquee in your garden? DIY weddings require a lot of coordination and a planner, or day-of coordinator will be worth their weight in gold.

### Are there two of you in it?
Stereotypes would have us believe that menfolk aren't interested in planning and ladies get lumped with all the work, but it's mostly not the case in our experience. If you are planning alone and aren't too happy about it, a planner might prevent the inevitable tension that will cause.

# CHOOSING YOUR WEDDING PARTY
## The Golden Rules

**Take your time**
In the excitement, it can be tempting to ask every close friend you tell about your engagement to be in your bride tribe. Hold fire until you've had a chance to mull over all the options. Ask yourself, will I still be as close to this person in five years' time?

**What kind of bride/groom are you?**
Before you decide who'll make a good bridesmaid, ask yourself what you need. Do you want some fun gal pals to get excited with and have one hell of a hen? Or do you crave a reliable team of co-planners?

**Don't rule anyone out based on their gender**
Tradition brings with it some lovely rituals, but it shouldn't dictate that your best male friend can't be in your wedding party, alongside your 'maids. And we think that fab, female friend will make a deadly best woman.

**Do I have to ask her, just because she asked me?**
Whilst it would be ideal to always return the favour, you might have been a bridesmaid for three or four friends already and you can't ask everyone, particularly if you also have a gaggle of sisters. So no, it's not the rule, but manage expectations by communicating openly about it.

**Include your siblings**
Your siblings are your mates for life (even if you kill each other sometimes), so try to include them in your wedding party, if you can.

**A lopsided wedding party is A-OK**
Your wedding party is not a set of accounts – it doesn't have to balance. If your other half asked his or her two best friends but you really want four groomsmen or bridesmaids, it's really no biggie.

**You don't have to have one!**
Maybe you think you and your sister will manage just fine or you don't have the budget to dress five fabulous females. That's perfectly fine – wedding tradition is not the boss of you.

# Confetti loves...
## SELECTED SUPPLIERS

**STYLED BY AMBER**
STYLEDBYAMBERIS@GMAIL.COM
STYLEDBYAMBER.COM

**HOLLIE THE WEDDING PLANNER**
TEL: 0034 6932 63729
HOLLIETHEWEDDINGPLANNER.COM

**FIELDS**
TEL: 01 477 9000
FIELDS.IE

# Getting started notes

# The Venue

## EVERYTHING IN ITS PLACE

# This Must Be The Place

When it comes to wedding planning, we advise getting 'the big three' out of the way first, by securing your date with your dream venue, awesome band and top-notch photographer. But the reality is that your venue is the biggest of all planning aspects. After all, it determines the vibe and flow of your day and how the whole event will look. Your venue comes with a team of people that will form part of your wedding family for the next few months and the place will come to mean the world to you, for ever more. It's not just step one, it's more like steps one through ten.

So how do you make such a big decision? The easiest way to start is with a process of elimination. After you've decided on your guest list and budget, rule out anything that doesn't fit both and move the hell on. No beautiful, winding driveway or period feature will change the fact that a particular venue is not big enough for your numbers or way out of your price range.

After that, it's time to determine your priorities. Is it important for you to marry in the county your folks came from? Is it vital for you that all your guests can stay together for the weekend? In this chapter, we chat about choosing your venue, the types of reception spaces and ceremonies available in Ireland; about making your ceremony completely unique to you and the ins and outs of church weddings in Ireland, should you choose to go down that route.

Like all planning aspects, venue hunting is what you make of it. Weekends spent viewing potential premises don't have to feel like hassle. Look at them as exciting road trips with your betrothed, full of possibility. Once you've found 'the one', you'll probably feel drawn to visit it lots before the day too.

*Happy hunting!*

# Types Of Venue

When it comes to Irish weddings, one size does not fit all. Luckily, we're spoiled for choice with a huge variety of venues to choose from, covering all sizes and styles of weddings. These are the main types to consider...

### Traditional/Hotel
**Pros** There's usually ample accommodation for all of your guests and every need can be catered for by experienced staff who are used to large numbers of guests.

**Cons** Putting your own stamp on the venue can be more of a challenge, but it's infinitely doable.

### Stately Home/Castle
**Pros** Full of character and history; it's often a real treat for you and your guests to visit and stay in such historic buildings.

**Cons** The dining room may not be large enough for your reception, making a marquee necessary. There may not be enough accommodation for all of your guests.

### Alternative
**Pros** Your wedding will feel very unique - brilliant if you've attended a lot of friends' weddings in recent years and equally great for your multiple wedding-going guests.

**Cons** It may be extra work to get the venue ready for large numbers.

### City venue
**Pros** Every facility is on your doorstep and it offers unique, urban photo opportunities.

**Cons** You might miss out on that feeling of everyone being away together for the weekend.

### Home/DIY venue
**Pros** It can be whatever you want it to be and nobody else will have been married there, making it uniquely yours.

**Cons** Constructing a venue from the ground up is a lot of work – *check out our handy list on page 38 for everything you'll need to arrange.*

# Making A Venue Your Own

Most couples crave that elusive 'something different' and want their wedding and venue to be unique and perfectly them, so what do you do about those niggling venue worries? Here are the most common concerns and potential pitfalls and, most importantly, how to overcome them.

**"I hate the carpet!"**
There is a certain 'hotel carpet' look and, let's face it, it's not to everyone's taste. But unless you visit your venue during a wedding fair, the reception space is likely to be quite bare, so that carpet you don't like is probably far more prominent now than it will be on the day. Try to picture the room fully dressed – after all, you're probably going to fit as many tables as possible into the room, so the carpet will be all but covered anyway. Also, the lighting is likely to be far more atmospheric and forgiving. If all else fails, adding height and drama to the reception room with hired faux cherry blossoms or towering candelabras should do the trick.

**"I hate the chairs!"**
If you don't like the chairs at your chosen venue, the obvious answer is chair covers, but they're not to everyone's taste either. Hiring chairs is the way forward, but this can be a pricey business. This expense, however, is worth it. Chairs form a very prominent part your décor, so if your budget will stretch to it, hire pieces you love. Try Gotcha Covered (*gotchacovered.ie*), Frog Prince Weddings & Events (*frogprince.ie*) or CaterHire (*caterhire.ie*).

**"I'm worried the venue will be full of non-wedding guests."**
If the venue of your dreams isn't private hire, there will be people on the grounds that aren't at your wedding. However, this doesn't have to be a negative. Venues are used to ensuring ceremonies are completely private and making sure that wedding parties get the very best treatment. Passers-by will wish you well with a smile and you might find that it's actually lovely being the centre of attention for the day.

**"I'm worried it will be the same as my friend's wedding."**
If a friend or family member married at the same venue, you might worry that your guests will compare your days. That's unlikely to be the case - they're your friends and will just be delighted to be there. But you obviously don't want an identikit wedding. Speak to your venue about switching things up. Can you have your ceremony outside? Opt for long tables instead of round? Have a gourmet buffet instead of the regular meal? Simple things such as changing the running order will separate your day from theirs. Try having your speeches after the ceremony, during your drinks reception, for example.

# Types Of Ceremony

If you're not religious, there are plenty of ceremony options available to you, including civil, humanist and spiritual. Here's our complete guide to each...

## Civil

Civil ceremonies are performed by civil registrars from Monday to Friday. Registrars will only perform ceremonies outside the registry office on certain days at certain times, and it may come at an extra cost - it varies from county to county. You'll register with the registrar of the county in which you intend to marry. If you wish to marry at your reception venue, make sure to check that it's licensed for civil ceremonies - most are now. Your venue will need to be a fixed structure (or part of), so you cannot marry on a beach, cliff or in a forest, unless it's part of the grounds of your chosen venue. For more information on civil ceremonies, see *citizensinformation.ie* or *welfare.ie*

## Humanist

A humanist wedding ceremony is a secular celebration with a flexible format, influenced heavily by the couple. You have the option of including poetry, music, personal vows, readings, and personal traditions. Celebrants will provide templates that you can alter to suit you both and your vision for the day. You will still need to give the Civil Registrar of Marriage a minimum of three months' notice before you marry. To discuss arrangements and the details of a humanist ceremony, get in touch with a celebrant directly. For information on humanist celebrants, see *humanism.ie*

## Spiritual

A spiritual wedding ceremony is a non-denominational ceremony that doesn't conform to any one set of mainstream religious beliefs. Everything in a spiritualist ceremony can be tailored to you and your partner, making it a personal celebration about the two of you. It is a spiritualist's belief that you can invite those from the spirit world to be present on the day, and they will remember those who have passed. There are various elements you can incorporate, such as the lighting of candles, traditional hand fasting, a rose ceremony and sand ceremony - where each person has an individual vessel of sand which they pour together into a larger vessel to symbolise the unity of two families. For more information on spiritual ceremonies, visit *spiritualceremonies.ie*

# Religious Ceremonies
## EVERYTHING YOU NEED TO KNOW

### Finding a priest/vicar

Priests/vicars can refuse to marry a couple they do not know or couples that aren't of their religion, so be sure to approach one as soon as possible. If you wish to have a priest/vicar whom you know (but is not from the parish where you hope to marry) perform the ceremony, this will have to be discussed with the local parish priest/vicar. You will need their permission to use the church if another member of the clergy is to perform a marriage ceremony there. Traditionally the priest/vicar is also invited to the reception, but it's less of a requirement now.

### Booking a church

If you wish to get married in your local parish church, you must first arrange a meeting with your local priest/vicar to confirm a date and other details. Keep in mind that marriage ceremonies won't be performed on religious holidays such as Good Friday, St. Patrick's Day, Christmas Day etc. If you aren't from the area, policies for marrying non-locals will vary from church to church. Our advice is to draw up a shortlist of two or three churches in the area, in case your first choice doesn't work out. There will be a fee for use of the church on the day which can range from €200 right up to €500, depending on the parish. Church flowers, if you wish to have them, will be left up to you to organise through your chosen florist. It's often expected that they are left in the church after the ceremony.

### Timeline

You'll need to confirm details such as date, church, priest/vicar at least three months prior to your wedding. Even though you're having a religious ceremony, your marriage must first be registered with the state. Meet with a Civil Registrar of Marriage a minimum of three months before your wedding, in order to get your Marriage Registration Form (MRF). This is essentially your marriage licence and will cost you approximately €200. *Read more about this on page 12.*

# YOU ARE THE MAGIC
You're right where
# I WANNA BE

*Michael McDonald*

# Making Your Ceremony Unique

Who says your reception has to be the only fun part? Religious restrictions aside, there's no reason why your ceremony can't be as inventive and unique as the party that follows.

**Get to know your celebrant**
Infusing your love story into proceedings is a lovely, easy way to personalise the day. Your celebrant will lead your ceremony, so meet with them a few times before your wedding to let them get to know your personalities. Incorporating some fun anecdotes about you both will instantly add personality and help guests feel more connected to the two of you.

**Include meaningful readings**
From religious passages and songs to old love letters or even texts to one another, there are lots of places you can pull your readings from. Invite your loved ones to read your chosen passages. Alternatively, if you have a friend with a talent for spoken word, singing or even playing guitar, ask them to perform something that will be totally unique for your day. Including readings from your parents' weddings is also a lovely touch – make sure to let your guests know the meaning behind it.

**Write your own vows**
To have and to hold, for better or for worse is all well and good, but writing your own wedding vows is a surefire way to make your wedding ceremony your own. It's a declaration of your love and commitment to each other and pouring your hearts into it will help your guests to feel invested in it too.

**Something old...**
Include traditions that feel significant and relevant to you as a couple and/or ones that symbolically blend your families together, such as a unity candle or rose ceremony. Carry on family traditions, such as grandparents or parents giving a blessing, or incorporate traditions from your culture or heritage. This is a lovely way to honour your relationship, families and where you both come from.

**Get your guests involved**
Getting everyone involved will create an intimate feel for your ceremony. Have a family and friends vow before your own vows, where your guests respond to a communal vow to show their support for you. Or, before you exchange your wedding rings, have a ring-warming ceremony, where friends and family pass your rings around so everyone can offer their good vibes to you, while your celebrant tells your story.

# Getting Married At Home

If you've got a particularly lovely home, or have a special place in mind to marry, there are some things you will need to consider. We've compiled our ultimate list of DIY venue considerations...

### Celebrant
Marry Me Ireland (*marrymeireland.ie*) offers a wide array of celebrants who will work with you to create a ceremony that reflects you as a couple.

### Marquee
A marquee is a great idea for extra room or, if you're planning an outdoor garden party, for shelter from the elements. Try The Outdoor Wedding Company (*outdoorweddingcompany.ie*), Extreme Structures (*extremestructures.ie*), LPM Bohemia (*lpmbohemia.com*), Tipi Faoi Na Réaltaí (*tipifaoinarealtai.ie*) or Magnakata (*magnakata.com*) for options.

### Power
You may need generators for lights and heaters. Companies such as Generator Hire (*generatorhire.ie*) can sort you out.

### Lighting
This can include fairy lights, festoon lights or bigger overhead lights, depending on the vibe you're going for and how well lit the area is already.

### Toilets
Take the amount of guests into consideration - if your house only has one or two loos, hiring some in is the way forward. Rather than a standard portaloo, opt for something like VIP Luxury Loos (*vipluxuryloos.com*).

### Furniture/Tablewear
For a slap-up shindig at home, you'll need to hire a wide range of items like cutlery, glasses, plates, chairs and bar set ups. Companies like CaterHire have a huge selection to choose from (*caterhire.ie*).

### Décor
If you're going all DIY, rally the troops and get your bridal party or friends to give you a hand decorating the space.

*"Hiring a professional cleaning
company is a good idea, so you can
enjoy the celebrations without too
much hard work"*

## Alcohol
Whether you plan on stocking a full, free bar or just wine and bottled beer, you'll need enough to ensure you don't run out.

## Catering
Assuming that you won't be slaving away in the kitchen cooking your guests' meals, you'll need caterers. There are plenty of professional catering companies in Ireland who will offer the full experience, including staff to wait the tables. Check out Andrew Holmes Catering (*andrewholmescatering.ie*), Eunice Power Catering (*eunicepower.com*) and Turning Tables Dining (*turningtablesdining.ie*).

## Permission
If you live in a built-up area, you will need to clear it with the people around you first, before you make some noise.

## Cleaning
Your caterers will usually clear away all things food related, but there will still be lots to clean up. Hiring a professional cleaning company is a good idea, so you can enjoy the celebrations without too much hard work.

## Plan B
What if there's torrential rain on the day? Do you have a back-up plan? If your house is big enough to sustain your guests, you can move everything indoors. If not, look into getting a more sturdy marquee structure with flooring and heating.

# QUESTIONS TO ASK YOUR VENUE BEFORE YOU BOOK

## Pricing and availability

1. Is my ideal date available? If not, what are the surrounding dates that are free?
2. Do you offer different rates for mid-week versus weekend?
3. What packages are on offer and what's included in each?

## Payment

1. How much is the deposit and how soon does it need to be paid?
2. What's the payment breakdown like?
3. What's your cancellation policy?
4. What is the latest date for changes to menu, adding extra guests etc?

## Vendors

1. Do you have a list of recommended vendors?
2. Can we use our own choice of vendors?
3. Is it possible to bring in any extras such as lawn games or an ice-cream van?

## Food and drink

1. Can you facilitate food in-house or will we need to hire in caterers?
2. Is there a minimum number of guests needed for the meal?
3. Can we bring our own wine for the meal? If so, is there a corkage fee?

## Logistics

1. Is the venue wheelchair accessible?
2. Are there noise restrictions? If so, what are they?
3. How late can we party that night?
4. Is there ample parking onsite?
5. Do we need to hire in extra toilet facilities? (For alternative venues)

## Specifics

1. What's the total capacity?
2. How many weddings do you host per day?
3. Do you have your own sound equipment for our band/DJ?
4. Can we have our ceremony onsite?
5. If so, is it possible to have an outdoor ceremony and is there a backup plan if it's raining?
6. Are there any décor restrictions?
7. When can our vendors arrive to set up on the day?
8. Will your staff be involved in the set-up and breaking down, or will we need to organise this ourselves?

# Confetti loves...
## SELECTED SUPPLIERS

**BELLE ISLE CASTLE & PRIVATE ISLAND**
TEL: +44 28 6638 7231
BELLE-ISLE.COM

**BALLYMAGARVEY VILLAGE**
TEL: 041 982 5959
BALLYMAGARVEY.IE

**DROMOLAND CASTLE**
TEL: 061 368 144
DROMOLAND.IE

**DUNBOYNE CASTLE**
TEL: 01 801 3500
DUNBOYNECASTLEHOTEL.COM

**BARBERSTOWN CASTLE**
TEL: 01 628 8157
BARBERSTOWNCASTLE.IE

**HORETOWN HOUSE**
TEL: 051 565633
HORETOWNHOUSE.IE

Image: Wojciech Koza Photography

**COOLBAWN QUAY**
COOLBAWNQUAY.COM
INSTAGRAM: @coolbawnquay

**KILSHANE HOUSE**
TEL: O62 82444
KILSHANEHOUSE.IE

**THE JOHNSTOWN ESTATE**
TEL: 046 954 0000
THEJOHNSTOWNESTATE.COM

**CASTLEMARTYR RESORT**
TEL: 021 421 9000
CASTLEMARTYRRESORT.IE

**CLANARD COURT WEDDINGS**
TEL: 059 8640 666
CLANARDCOURT.IE

**MARKREE CASTLE**
TEL: 071 916 7800
ROMATICCASTLESIRELAND.IE

**KINNITTY CASTLE HOTEL**
TEL: 057 913 7318
KINNITTYCASTLEHOTEL.COM

**TULFARRIS HOTEL & GOLF RESORT**
TEL: 045 867 600
TULFARRISHOTEL.COM

# Venue notes

# Fashion

## IN THIS AWESOME DRESS, I THEE WED

# Saying Yes To The Dress

Shopping for your wedding dress is like no other retail experience; logistically, emotionally and certainly financially, it's a whole new ballgown. And here's something they don't tell you – not everyone enjoys the process. That elusive, tearful moment when you try on the dress you've been dreaming of, surrounded by your 'maids and Mam and instantly know it's the one... that might never happen. Sometimes, instead, it begins as a frustratingly fruitless search, dispenses as many disappointments as delights and culminates in one very difficult decision. The pay off? Once you find it, your dress will become the new love of your life and finding 'the one' will be worth every second.

In this chapter, we break down gown shopping in an attempt to demystify the process. Our aim is to make it a less daunting undertaking and one that you'll enjoy. We'll cover timelines, styles and shapes, tell you what to expect when you visit boutiques, and what (and who) to bring with you. You're also probably hearing a whole new dictionary of words right now, so if you want to know your bustle from your bodice and your Juliet sleeve from your fingertip veil, read on. There's no exam at the end, but it's helpful to know what your options are and, most importantly, what to ask for.

Of course, it's not just yourself you have to dress; traditionally speaking, you'll be forking out for fab frocks for your fave gals too. That brings its own share of challenges, so we're answering the big questions about bridesmaids and offering our best advice for smooth sailing.

And what about the lads? Once you delve into the world of groomswear, you suddenly realise that a suit is not just a suit. Two or three pieces? Morning suits or black tie? Our helpful breakdown of suits by type should steer you in the right direction and we'll answer the most frequently asked groomsmen's fashion questions too.

Our best fashion advice, however, is to remember on every shopping outing that this, right here, is your wedding. Your wedding is now – not just the day itself. So, make every activity an event and enjoy it all (even if it's not exactly going to plan!) After all, these days out with your pals and parents are the days you'll miss when the final cork has popped and the thank you cards are sent.

*Happy shopping!*

# Wedding Fashion Checklist

When creating your wedding budget, it's easy to overlook the smaller details. This is the number one reason nearly-weds go over cost. So, don't forget about these wedding fashion essentials when you're doing your sums.

## Veil
Depending on what style or brand you go for, this could set you back a few hundred euro, so make sure it's allowed for in the budget.

## Shoes
The temptation to splash out on some designer heels might be too much, so make sure you can afford them before you hand over that credit card.

## Bag
You'll need a small bag for your essentials on the day.

## Alterations
Costs for these vary greatly but you're looking at shelling out somewhere between €100 and €250.

## Underwear
Your dress might require the perfect strapless bra or seamless, nude undies.

## Lingerie
Your wedding day underwear might be more functional than flattering, so if you want to buy something gorgeous for your wedding night or honeymoon, it's one more item to pop on the list.

## Jewellery
Whether it's the perfect wedding day earrings, or a simple cuff.

## Accessories
Allow for that stunning, beaded belt or sparkling clips to jazz up your shoes.

## A fab 'rehearsal' dress
The the last thing you'll need the day before your wedding is an outfit decision, so plan it in advance.

## A day two outfit
Remember, you're still the star of the show on day two. A cute, white midi dress, or jumpsuit works a treat.

## Pretty pyjamas
This is something you'll regret not picking up when you see your wedding morning pics. Don't forget some pretty slippers too.

## Honeymoon clothes
Don't leave this until the last minute and remember smart airport attire, newlyweds have a far better chance of an upgrade if they're dressed neatly.

## Something old, new, borrowed and blue
Your fashion choices are a great way to incorporate these traditional items. Blue shoes, anyone?

# WEDDING DRESS SHOPPING
## The Timeline

### 12 MONTHS TO GO:
### SET YOUR BUDGET
Decide how much you're willing to spend and remember to budget for alterations and accessories.

### DO YOUR RESEARCH
Study styles you like and shapes that suit your figure.

### CHOOSE YOUR ENTOURAGE
Decide who's on your dress dream team and find out what dates they're free.

### 6 MONTHS TO GO:
### CHOOSE YOUR ACCESSORIES
Headpiece or veil? Buy two pairs of shoes - a change is as good as a rest.

### 6 WEEKS TO GO:
### BREAK IN YOUR SHOES
Try our 'two socks trick' - wear one pair and pop another on over your shoes, loosening the fit whilst protecting them from scuffing.

### HAVE YOUR FINAL FITTING
Time to see the finished product!

### 10 MONTHS TO GO:
### BOOK YOUR APPOINTMENTS
Nine months out is the ideal time to start, but it might take a couple of weeks to get an appointment.

### 9 MONTHS TO GO:
### SHOP FOR UNDIES
A great strapless bra or some smart shapewear can completely change your opinion of a dress.

### START SHOPPING
Don't be overwhelmed - obey the 'rule of three'. Book three appointments and, if you haven't found the one, book three more.

### 3 MONTHS TO GO:
### YOUR FIRST FITTING
Any major alterations happen now - like adding sleeves or neckline changes. We love Anna O Alterations. (alterationsannao.com)

### 2 WEEKS TO GO:
### COLLECT YOUR DRESS
Store it in a breathable, opaque garment bag.

# WEDDING DRESS SHOPPING
## 10 Things You Need To Know

**1. Early bird**
Start your style research up to a year before your wedding, so you have some idea what you're looking for. Book your appointments in advance – it might take a few weeks to get a weekend appointment in your chosen boutiques during busy season. Your appointments should take place around nine months before the wedding to allow enough time for your chosen dress to arrive and for the fittings and alterations process.

**2. Talkin' about money**
Be sure to let the bridal boutique know your budget as soon as you arrive. Trying on dresses way out of your price range will only lead to heartache.

**3. Fail to prepare, prepare to fail**
Research is vital and will save you precious time at appointments. Scour Pinterest, Instagram and *confetti.ie* for different styles, shapes and colours. Also, research the designers each store holds and find out which styles they stock from their collections.

**4. Open your mind**
Be open to suggestion and try on a few different styles at your first appointment. Wedding dresses look completely different on the hanger and you might end up loving something you never imagined yourself in.

**5. Too many cooks…**
Don't bring your entire wedding party to your appointments – we can't stress this enough. We've all seen those episodes of *Say Yes To The Dress*, with a stressed-out bride listening to ten opinionated pals. We recommend a maximum of three people.

**6. Take the weight off your mind**
Buy a dress that fits now – regardless of any weight-loss plans. Ordering a dress in a much smaller size, hoping it will fit on the day, is one of the most common mistakes brides make and adds enormous pressure to proceedings. Remember, it's much easier to take a wedding dress in, than it is to let it out.

### 7. Accessorise all areas

Come armed! Many boutiques will have shoes to try on, but it's better to have a pair that are the same height as those you plan to wear on the day. Nude underwear, shapewear and a strapless bra are key too - so you'll get the full effect and can make a better call.

### 8. Tick tock

Use your time wisely as you'll probably only have an hour at each appointment. That sounds like plenty of time, but in reality it translates into trying on around four to six dresses. If you don't know what you're looking for, it'll feel shorter again, so don't dilly-dally. (This is another reason not to bring a huge gang with you!)

### 9. Know your stuff

Leave the boutique armed with the vital information you need. How long will your dress take to arrive? Does the boutique offer an alteration service and, if so, what are the timelines and fees involved? If not, who do they recommend?

### 10. Know the one that's one too many

Found your gown? Stop shopping. Continuing to browse after you've found 'the one' will only wreck your head. Move on to other exciting planning elements and anticipate your first fitting!

I TALKED TO YOUR DAD,
GO PICK OUT A

*white dress*

IT'S A LOVE STORY,
BABY JUST SAY YES

Taylor Swift

# WEDDING DRESS STYLES BY BODY SHAPE

Brides come in many glorious shapes and sizes, so the first important step is establishing the right style for your unique shape.

## Hourglass

If you've got the curves, girl, show 'em off! Figure-hugging mermaid or trumpet-style gowns really accentuate your shape, nipping you in at the waist and flowing over your shapely silhouette. Fuller ballgown styles or ruffles and tiers may not do your frame justice.

## Athletic/boyish

If your figure is a little on the straight side, introduce some shape with added volume and detailing around the hips and chest. Try on A-line, ballgown or empire-line styles – these will help balance your frame and create the illusion of an hourglass silhouette. Avoid strapless gowns or skinny straps that can make shoulders appear broader.

## Inverted triangle

If your shoulders are wider than your lower body, opt for V-neck gowns with thicker straps or sleeves. Styles to avoid are halternecks and off-the-shoulder gowns.

## Apple

If you have a fuller bust and straight hips, try classic A-line styles or full ballgowns that nip you in, accentuating the smallest part of your waist. Avoid high necklines, opting instead for a V-neck or scooped neckline dresses.

## Fuller chest

If you've got a fuller chest but don't want straps, we recommend going for an off-the-shoulder or Bardot style, instead of entirely strapless. Also, a nipped-in waistline will help to define your shape even more.

## Smaller chest

Brides with smaller busts should avoid sweetheart necklines, opting instead for a straight or high neck. Having a smaller chest gives you lots of options, including halterneck and backless, as less support is needed.

## Petite

Simplicity is key for petite brides. An elegant sheath gown will create one long line and elongate your frame. High-low dresses will give the illusion of longer legs and an empire waist will draw the eye up the body, again creating a longer silhouette. Steer clear of fuller ballgowns, as they may overwhelm your smaller frame and, if you're going for a short dress, be careful about ballet length, opting instead for a dress that falls just below the knee.

## Pear

An A-line wedding dress is the perfect silhouette for pear-shaped ladies, as it will balance out fuller hips. Consider dresses with texture or detailing on top too.

# Wedding Gown Glossary

**Basque**
A dropped, V-shaped, fitted waist.

**Bateau neckline**
A round neckline that gently follows the curve of the collarbone.

**Bell sleeve**
A sleeve that's narrow at the armhole and tapers out to the wrist.

**Bias cut**
Cut diagonally.

**Brocade**
Heavy, woven fabric with raised design.

**Bustle**
Fabric added at the back, just below the waist, to add fullness.

**Court train**
Starts from the waist and trails about a foot behind the bride.

**Drop waist**
The waist sits at hip level.

**Empire line**
Nipped in just below the bust.

**Fishtail train**
Flares out seamlessly from the knee.

**High-low**
Short at the front, long at the back.

**Illusion back**
A sheer back panel.

**Juliet sleeve**
A long sleeve that's fitted at the wrist.

**Keyhole back**
A circular-shaped opening at the back.

**Organza**
A semi-sheer, stiff fabric.

**Overskirt**
A sometimes-detachable outer skirt, worn over the skirt.

**Peplum**
An overskirt attached at the waistline.

**Queen Anne neckline**
A high collar in the back and scoop in the front.

**Scoop neck**
A low, circular neckline.

**Sheath dress**
A simple, close-to-the-body style dress.

**Trumpet/Fit-and-flair**
Flares out at the knee.

**Tulle**
Fine netting, often made from silk.

**Watteau train**
A panel of fabric that falls from below the shoulder blades to the floor.

# VEILS BY TYPE

### Birdcage
The shortest veil, a birdcage is usually attached to an Alice band or hairclip. Styles vary, but generally some tulle or netting covers one or both eyes.

### Blusher
A blusher veil is traditionally worn over the face and is pushed back from the face after the ceremony.

### Fly-away
A shoulder length veil with multiple tiered layers of tulle. At their peak in the Sixties, they're quite retro now.

### Shoulder-length
Slightly longer than the fly-away and again reminiscent of the Sixties, it's a fun option often worn with shorter, informal dress styles.

### Elbow-length
An elbow-length veil works beautifully to gently cover your shoulders and frame the face.

### Fingertip
The fingertip veil falls to arms' length and is a great option for brides who want the drama of a long veil and the freedom to move without restriction.

### Ballet-length
Also known as a Waltz, the ballet-length veil falls somewhere between your fingertips and the floor. It's ideal for those windswept veil shots.

### Chapel length
A chapel-length veil is the same length as your dress, or a little longer and usually made from simple, sheer tulle so back detail is still visible.

### Cathedral length
A cathedral veil's length extends beyond the length of your dress, for regal drama. It's the most formal of lengths but comes in many styles to suit lots of different dresses.

### Mantilla
This Spanish-inspired veil is made from lace and often features a detailed, scalloped edge, worn around the face.

### Juliet cap
Named after the Shakespearean heroine, a Juliet Cap is a small open-work cap worn on top of the head with a long veil attached to the back.

# The Big Questions, Answered

**Who pays for what?**
In Irish weddings, the couple generally buys dresses for their bridesmaids. If you're asking them to wear a particular pair of shoes or specific accessories, it's customary to pay for those too. However, if they have free rein over how they accessorise, it's okay to ask them to pick up their own.

**How much should I budget?**
This depends on your overall spend. If you're going for high street finds you might start at around the €100 mark. After that, the sky's the limit.

**Do they all have to wear the same?**
It's becoming more popular to choose complementary dresses, instead of matching ones. A similar dress in different colours works well, as does the same shade in different shapes. Completely mismatched 'maids are also more than acceptable and can be a really fun, laidback approach.

**What if they're all different shapes?**
If you want to cater for everyone, but are craving uniformity, opt for different dresses in the same colour.

**What if one of my bridesmaids is pregnant?**
Multi-way wrap dresses are popular for bridesmaids, for all the reasons mentioned above and they're also suitable for pregnant bridesmaids. Try brands such as Eliza & Ethan, Dessy and twobirds.

**What if one (or all) of them is very fussy?**
Narrow your selection down to three dresses and let them decide amongst themselves which one they'll go for. Remove yourself from the discussion at this point and let them come back to you with an answer.

**How far in advance of the wedding should we shop?**
Six to eight months in advance gives you plenty of time, and leaves plenty of time for alterations and accessorising the look.

**What if one of my bridesmaids lives abroad?**
Start early, but it's not as much hassle as it sounds. If the brand you're going for is available where she lives, send her on a solo trying-on mission. If not, you might need to post the dress to her in advance and let her look after any alterations.

**What if they have expensive tastes?**
Make your budget clear at the start. If one, or all, of your bridesmaids finds something outside that, they always have the option of adding the extra to it – it's not uncommon.

# SHOPPING FOR BRIDESMAIDS
## A Guide To Plain Sailing

### You first!
Choose your gown first, as this will often determine the style and colour of your bridesmaids' dresses. You don't want to find yourself having to work it the other way around!

### Research it
Having a couple of specific dresses in mind is a great start. Remember, the boutique won't necessarily have every style in a specific collection, so have a look on their website and Facebook pages.

### Pre-gaming
Chatting before you start leads to a far more focused search. Give each bridesmaid a veto card - for example, if your redhead bestie simply won't wear pink or your petite sister will feel swamped in a ballgown style.

### Time after time
Before you kick off, set a reasonable schedule. Plan to have made your final decision within a month and stick to it.

### Size matters
Avoid ordering in smaller sizes, no matter how much anyone insists they're 'shredding for the wedding'. You can always have the dress taken in, but avoid the headache and awkwardness of something not fitting closer to the day.

### Be season saavy
Having a winter wedding? High street shopping trips during the summer months are not going to deliver sparkly evening gowns. Be super clever and pick up your dresses in the post-Christmas sale earlier on in the year.

### Don't take it personally
Someone having a strop in a shop? Take a deep breath and try to understand why she's frustrated. Chances are, she's feeling the pressure of things not fitting or looking great on her. Regular breaks to regroup are a great idea - make them Prosecco pitstops and you have yourself a party.

### Come prepared
Much like your own dress shopping trips, asking your 'maids to wear appropriate underwear and shoes gives a far better chance of everyone looking and feeling good.

### Make it an event!
Your 'maids might be a little anxious starting out on this dress hunt. What if the other gals love one dress and she hates it? What if they feel fat in everything they try on? Making a lovely day out of proceedings will relax everyone. Plan afternoon tea for after your trip or visit another city and stay overnight to shop. Road trip!

## TOP TIPS

### The right NOT to bare arms

Let's be real here, how many of your mates like their arms? On your average night out, who amongst them wears a strapless, or even sleeveless, dress or top? We're willing to bet the number is low. So why presume they'll be happy in a halter all of a sudden? So many bridesmaids' dresses have a scary sweetheart neckline or the demon capped sleeve – SCREAM! Deciding from the get-go that you're after a style with sleeves will make the majority instantly happy and make for a much happier experience all round.

### A game of two halves

More bridesmaids in tops and skirts, we say! It's a far more forgiving sartorial situation for most frames and opens up a whole world of choice. And, if you're mixing things up with different shades and shapes, this is definitely the easiest way to do it. This will also give you more options in terms of which boutiques to visit. For high street options, we love stores like Folkster (*folkster.com*) and online shops like ASOS (*asos.com*), which both have a beautiful selection of formal skirts and elegant tops that will do the trick.

# GROOMSWEAR AND GROOMSMEN'S FASHION
## The Big Questions, Answered

**Should groomsmen wear a different suit to the groom?**
Strictly speaking, yes. Groomsmen's suits should complement the groom's, but not match.

**Should the groomsmen match the bridesmaids in some way?**
It's not uncommon for the groomsmen's accessories to give a nod to the colours chosen for the bridesmaids. If you're taking the traditional approach, the overall palette of the wedding party will be somewhat cohesive.

**To hire or buy?**
This often depends on how formal the wedding is. If you're going for a laid-back tweed or herringbone look for the guys, buying is often an affordable option. But if yours is a formal or black-tie affair, renting tuxes or morning suits may make more sense. Often, a couple will purchase the groom's suit to ensure it's the perfect fit and style and rent suits for the groomsmen.

**How far in advance of the wedding should suit fittings take place?**
If you're buying your suit, have your first fitting at least three months before the wedding. Try to make your last fitting as near to the wedding date as possible, in case of any weight fluctuation.

**What are the timelines for renting?**
Make an appointment a couple of months before the wedding or, if you're marrying at peak season, consider going earlier to ensure the full selection of suit styles and sizing is available.

**How soon after the wedding do rentals need to be brought back?**
This is a job for the best man. Make sure he gathers up everyone's outfits before they leave your venue. Generally, suit hire companies will give you a couple of days to return suits rented for a wedding, but always check to avoid paying late fees.

# Suits By Type

Before you decide on the sartorial POA, you'll need to establish what kind of wedding you're having. Is it a formal, black-tie affair or a rustic barn wedding? This will determine the overall vibe, before you get into specifics.

## FORMAL

### Tuxedo

A tuxedo is your classic, black evening suit. Complete with bow tie, satin-striped trousers and an optional cummerbund, it's the perfect choice for a formal, black-tie wedding.

### Morning suit

The morning suit is a more traditional choice and features a tailcoat, waistcoat and trousers. Tradition dictates that it's worn for early weddings, at noon or early afternoon, after which you'd switch to white tie and tails.

### White tie and tails

The evening equivalent of a morning suit, this is as formal as it gets with some grooms even opting for a top hat - fancy! It's a look that's rarely seen in Ireland and is all kinds of *My Fair Lady*.

## CASUAL OCCASION

### Modern day suit

A smart, yet laidback two-piece suit complete with tie is the ideal choice if your wedding is a chilled-out, informal event.

### Three-piece suit

A step up from a casual suit, consisting of a jacket, waistcoat and trousers, the three-piece suit gives off vintage vibes and is a touch smarter than a two-piece option.

### Waistcoat and bow tie

A three-piece suit, minus the jacket, gives a contemporary, laid-back vibe. It'll fit right in at an outdoor, summer celebration or festival-inspired do.

**TOP TIPS**

**Practice makes perfect**
Don't leave it until your wedding morning to tie a bow-tie for the first time! YouTube has plenty of tutorials to help you perfect it in advance.

**All tied up**
If you're wearing a necktie, make sure it's tied to the correct length. The general rule of thumb is that the tip of your tie should meet the middle of your belt buckle.

# Confetti loves...
## SELECTED SUPPLIERS

**LA BELLA SPOSA**
TEL: 01 807 5712
LABELLASPOSA.IE

**ANNA O ALTERATIONS**
ALTERATIONSANNAO.COM
ANNAOALTERATIONS@GMAIL.COM

**MADE TO MEASURE - MAIRE FORKIN DESIGNS**
TEL: 086 172 1563
INFO@MAIREFORKIN.IE

# Fashion notes

........................................................................................................

........................................................................................................

........................................................................................................

........................................................................................................

........................................................................................................

........................................................................................................

........................................................................................................

........................................................................................................

........................................................................................................

........................................................................................................

........................................................................................................

........................................................................................................

........................................................................................................

........................................................................................................

........................................................................................................

........................................................................................................

........................................................................................................

........................................................................................................

........................................................................................................

........................................................................................................

........................................................................................................

........................................................................................................

# Photography

OH, SNAP!

# Picture This

There are many wonderful ways of capturing your wedding day on film, for you to remember and relive for ever more. We can't overstate just how much you're going to adore your wedding photos and movie. It's such an exciting day when your pictures are finally ready, or your video pings into your inbox. Expect tears, laughs and everything you felt on the day to come rushing back. It's magical.

You and your photographer are about to become pretty good pals, and that's a great thing. Don't be afraid to tell them what you want, but trust them - they know what they're doing. You might decide to have 'first look' pictures before the ceremony or forgo staged family shots altogether in favour of more casual snaps – ensure you choose a photographer who will suit your wants and, together, you'll form the perfect plan for the day.

If there was one piece of advice we could impart here, and we're sure wedding photographers the world over would echo our sentiments, it's to ask guests to be mindful of your photographer. There's no need for Aunty Margaret to stand in the aisle to take a phone snap of you when you enter the church - your photographer will get a much nicer one. Well, they would if Aunty Margaret would get out of the way. Similarly, with your speeches, first dance, cake cutting or any other important moments – a stray iPhone can ruin a shot quicker than you can say, "Please sit down, Aunty Margaret!"

If you're not a huge fan of having your photo taken, you're forgiven for feeling a bit wobbly about this part. There are plenty of couples like you, but don't be tempted to forgo wedding photography or treat it as anything but a priority. Remember, your wedding is not a photoshoot, so relax, breathe and enjoy the intimacy of your portrait session. *(There's much more about this on page 82.)* There are many styles of wedding photography and, if you opt for a reportage photographer, you may not even notice they're there for the most part. In this chapter we aim to help you decide which style is best for you, both in photography and videography.

*Happy researching!*

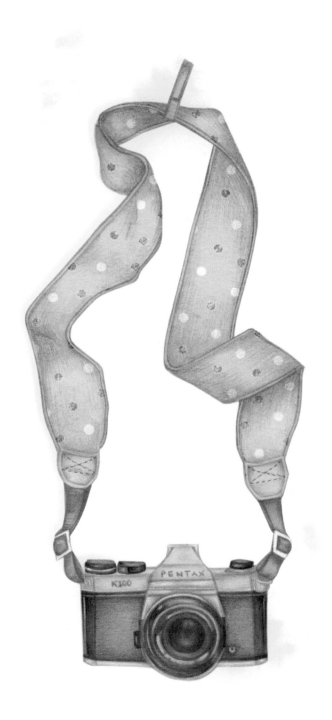

# HOW TO LOOK GREAT
## In Your Wedding Photos

**Pick a photographer you get on with**
Chances are you're not accustomed to being the focus of a professional photoshoot, so to avoid feeling uncomfortable on the day, make sure you feel relaxed around your photographer. They should be patient, make you feel calm, be able to break the tension with humour and most importantly, not be too intrusive. You'll know when you've met the right one. Try to meet up for coffee so your wedding day is not your first meeting. Or better still...

**Have an engagement shoot**
You might think they're a little cringey, but a practice run is always worth doing. It'll allow your photographer to get to know you and you'll be a pro by the time your wedding day rolls around. You need never show anyone the pictures (although we have a feeling you'll want to), but it's a great exercise for everyone involved. It's also a lovely, intimate thing to do when you don't have the pressure of a wedding day to worry about and often comes as part of a package with your photographer.

**Give yourself enough time**
Whilst nobody wants to miss too much of the party, make sure to allow ample time for your pictures.

Feeling rushed is one sure way of adding tension to proceedings and that will show in your posture and expressions. Allow at least 30 minutes for couple portraits and ensure your ceremony doesn't start late, as you're eating into this time.

**Focus on each other**
Staring at the camera like a bunny in headlights is never going to work. Direct your attention to your other half and pretend the camera's not there. Have a chat, tell each other a joke and have a cuddle. Maybe tell each other about your morning or what your favourite part of the ceremony was. Trust us - these are the pictures you'll cry over afterwards, knowing how happy and in love you both felt.

**Time it well**
Don't be a slave to regular wedding timelines. Your photographer will be able to advise when is the best time to sneak out for photos, depending on the time of year, location, and the weather that day. Bright sunlight is gorgeous for your drinks reception, but it will cast unflattering shadows and make it difficult not to squint. So enjoy your Pimms on the lawn with your pals and pop out during golden hour, before sunset, for warm flattering portraits instead.

## Go it alone

Having your wedding party around might make it more difficult to relax and let your guard down so, when it comes to your couple portraits, head off to somewhere secluded with your photographer for some 'alone time'. You'll get some great shots and it's a lovely opportunity to have some peace and quiet in the middle of the madness and magic of your wedding.

## Be comfortable

Having a comfortable dress will make your walk up the aisle, first dance, post-dinner boogie and photo time much easier. If you're constantly sucking in, or yanking up straps, you won't feel great. Similarly, your footwear will dictate where you can walk, how far and how easily. How you feel in what you're wearing will have a huge impact on your day.

# Practical Styling Tips

These simple visual steps will make your wedding look better instantly, without you having to pick up a craft scissors or inflate a single balloon.

### 1. Light it up
No matter how much you spend on that beautiful, big, wedding cake, if you place it in a dull corner of your reception space, it's not going to photograph beautifully. Always consider the light when placing key items. Your cake should be out of direct sunlight, but in a bright enough spot that all those lovely details can be picked up perfectly on camera. If the light is too artificial, that lovely pale blush frosting will look a gnarly shade of yellow in your photos. Visit your venue during daylight and choose where you'll put key items in advance. Similarly, if you're putting together a DIY photobooth or selfie station – ensure there's enough light so that all the Instagram snaps with your wedding hashtag on them are bright and colourful. Chances are you'll have your makeup done in a spot in your house or venue that has nice, natural light, so your 'getting ready' shots should be gorgeously lit by default. But remember to do the same when you're having your hair done. You'll be glad you did.

### 2. Hang tight
There's something really special about a stunning image of your dress, hanging expectantly before the big event. Your photographer will place it in good light to photograph it, but make sure you have something gorgeous to hang it on – there's nothing like a banjaxed wire coat hanger to ruin a perfectly good shot. The same goes for bridesmaids' dresses – hangers don't even need to be super fancy, but hanging everything on the same style of smart hanger will make for a more uniform and pleasing photo.

### 3. Invitation stations
A lot of couples tell us they wish they'd kept copies of their wedding invitations for themselves – they're a lovely keepsake and can look beautiful when framed in your home. Make sure you have a full set on hand on the morning of your wedding and ask your photographer to take some photos of the full suite.

### 4. Boxed off

Consider picking up a beautiful ring box to have your rings photographed in. It's a small touch that will give a professional styled look to the shot. We love The Sweetbee Box by Irish company, *bridetobee.ie*. Add in some flowers and a piece of your stationery and you have yourself an awesome wedding flatlay.

### 5. Something borrowed?

Remember to have your treasured wedding jewellery, particularly heirloom pieces or something you've borrowed from someone you love, photographed. Place them on a pretty trinket dish or old china plate for close ups, and ask your photographer to take a 'beauty shot' with those precious earrings on show or a close-up of your wrist with your Granny's bracelet on. You'll treasure these forever.

### 6. Clean up your act

This might sound very obvious, but when you're very busy in the lead up to your wedding, making sure your house is immaculate may not be at the top of your priority list. And, if you're getting ready at home, you might regret that box of Cornflakes on the counter or the washing drying on the radiator in the background of your images. If you don't have time and can afford it, consider having a professional cleaner in the day before, so your house is sparkling and you still have time to potter about to your final appointments. If ever there was a reason to spoil yourself, this is it.

AND IT'S THE SMALL THINGS
THAT MAKE ME SURE, LIKE HOW
we'd happily spend
hours on end
WITHOUT WORDS

The Coronas

# Wedding Photography
## WHAT YOU NEED TO KNOW

### The contract
A photography contract will prevent miscommunication and avoid any disappointment. Like any contract, it's important to make sure you know what you're signing. It will detail how much time your photographer will spend at your wedding; the number of photographs you'll receive; how you'll receive them; and what rights you have to the images. It'll also include timescales, details of cost, deposit, payment terms and cancellation policies. Keep a copy safe in case you have queries down the line about what was agreed.

### What you can expect to get
Packages will include an agreed number of hours and a password-protected online gallery from which you can download photos or order re-prints. A wedding album is usually an add-on. Most photographers provide 300-500 photos and you can expect edited digital files no sooner than six weeks after your wedding. In busy seasons like summer and Christmas, this may take considerably longer.

### On the day
Providing a traditional shot list is probably overkill – your photographer will know to shoot the important stuff. However, they won't know that you had an early date in the pub near your venue, or that the necklace you're wearing is a family heirloom that you'd love documented. Make a list of these important details.

By all means, take some essential group shots, but before you include 17 variations of parents and cousins, consider whether you'd put it in your wedding album. If the answer is no, don't waste your precious time rounding up the troops and go enjoy your cocktail reception.

### Approximate photography times
For the most part, photography will happen without you even noticing. However, there are certain things that will need to be scheduled in. If you're doing any of the below, here's how much time to allow for each.

◇ 20 mins – Dress on, final touches

◇ 20 mins – First look

◇ 20-30 mins – Bridal party portraits

◇ 20-30 mins – Family portraits

◇ 30 mins – Couple portraits

# STYLES OF WEDDING PHOTOGRAPHY

Once you've established your preferred style, finding
a wedding photographer will be a much easier job. Here are
four of the most popular styles...

## Traditional

A traditional wedding photographer appreciates the staples of a wedding and will capture them for you beautifully. Today, you can expect a modern take on the posed, formal photos in your grandparents' wedding album. The photographer will focus a lot on photos of the couple, groups and details, and will usually be quite involved in directing and guiding both you and the wedding party.

**Pros:** Timeless shots with no family member left out.

**Cons:** Portraits can take longer and you may miss some of the emotion.

## Fine art

Loosely speaking, fine art pushes past just documenting, into the more creative and artistic. It can be posed and constructed but the resulting photos are usually less formal than traditional photography. Fine art photographers shoot in film, often using unusual angles, interesting backdrops and extensive post-production techniques.

**Pros:** Beautiful photos that could be standalone art pieces.

**Cons:** You may not get every detail photo on your checklist.

## Photojournalistic/documentary /reportage

A style with many names, photojournalistic photographers unobtrusively capture your wedding as a whole, not just the planned moments. They aim to create a narrative, usually including more candid shots, full of genuine emotion. They capture the key elements of the day, but also focus on capturing the atmosphere.

**Pros:** Captures the emotion and story of the day.

**Cons:** May not cover extensive formal portraits unless you ask.

## Editorial

If you love the look of photography in fashion magazines, you can have your wedding shot in a similar style. Editorial photographers will shoot creatively, and will look to capture photos that are a little over the top, with dramatic backgrounds – perfect if you're marrying somewhere with dramatic landscapes or intense architecture. You won't find many candid shots in this style, but your formal shots will be more relaxed in feel because of the exciting lighting and angles.

**Pros:** Beautiful, artistic shots.

**Cons:** A danger of not capturing the real feel of the day.

# MUST-GET WEDDING PHOTOS

We recommend not over-instructing your photographer – they know what they're doing. However, if there's anything on the list that's an absolute MUST for you, let 'em know.

**Getting ready shots:** Your photographer should be quite unobtrusive when taking these photos, as it could be hectic in both camps. This will make for lovely, candid shots.

**Back shot:** If your dress has particularly lovely back detailing, this is vital – it'll also show off your presumably amazing hair style!

**Parents seeing you for the first time:** This is always one of our favourite shots. (No, you're crying!)

**Flatlay:** This is a gorgeous, more modern way of getting the perfect shot of your stationery, accessories and shoes. Ask your photographer, or someone from your bridal party, to set the shot up – or do it yourself if you have a particular vision in mind.

**Photo with both sets of parents/ grandparents:** If you're lucky enough to have them, this will prove to be a lovely keepsake for years to come.

**Awesome 'confetti' shot:** Whether it's emerging from your ceremony or on the dancefloor, be sure to have a confetti cannon or two on hand!

**The kiss:** This one's a no-brainer for photographers to capture.

**Couple portraits:** *Read all about how to nail these on page 82.*

**Venue shot:** If you have particular parts of the venue (both inside and out) you really love, let your photographer know.

**Bridal party:** Make them as posed or relaxed as you like – the more candid and fun the better, we say.

**Four-legged friends:** It's not always possible, but if you can have someone drop off your furry friend for photos, do it!

**Flowers:** Get a good shot of those pretty posies before you fling them at your mates later on.

**Guests:** At your drinks reception, your photographer will be in and around your guests, snapping away. It's so lovely to look back and see them all having a great time.

**The cake:** Have your cake set up on a styled table to make it picture perfect.

**Details:** This will include table plans, canapés, table settings and other décor items that you've added to the venue.

# QUESTIONS TO ASK YOUR WEDDING PHOTOGRAPHER **BEFORE** YOU BOOK

## Experience and availability

1. Is my wedding date available?
2. Have you ever worked at our venue before? If not, will you check it out in advance?
3. Can we see full galleries of a few of your recent weddings?
4. Will you be the one shooting my wedding, and will you have any assistants with you on our wedding day?
5. Will you be shooting any other weddings that weekend?

## Style

1. How would you describe your working style?
2. Do you prefer to blend into the background or do you tend to direct things more?
3. Are you willing to follow a shot list?
4. Do you shoot digitally, with film, or do you use both?
5. Do you shoot in colour, black and white, or both?

## Pricing and packages

1. What do your packages include and what will I have to pay extra for?
2. How much of a deposit is required to hold the date? When is the balance due?
3. How many hours are included in your packages? Do you charge overtime if things run over?
4. Is the album included in the price?

5. How many pictures will be taken and how many will we get to choose for our album?
6. How much retouching and colour correcting will you do on my images? Is there an extra charge?
7. Do you charge a travel fee? For what distance?

## Logistics

1. After the wedding, when can we expect to see the photos?
2. How will I receive my images?
3. Do I have the digital rights to my wedding photos?
4. What happens if you are ill or there's an emergency?
5. What information do you need from me before the wedding day?
6. What is your cancellation /refund policy?

# Do I Need A Videographer?

It's a question many couples ask themselves, when trying to save some cash. The short answer from us is a resounding YES!

While having both a photographer and videographer might feel a little extravagant, there's a danger that you'll regret not making it happen. In our recent wedding survey, 75% of people surveyed hired a wedding videographer. Of those who didn't, 100% said they regretted not doing so – a pretty telling statistic.

Your wedding photographer will, of course, capture your day perfectly and your photos will be beautiful and cherished. But video footage will help you relive moments over and over, and give you a bird's eye view of parts of the day you didn't even witness yourself. Photos are an amazing visual snapshot of the emotion and excitement of your wedding, while a video offers invaluable footage of your morning chats with family, the ceremony, the happy tears, speeches and everything else in between.

Previously, wedding videos were three hours long and only saw the light of day once a decade, but things have changed in a big way. Now you can opt for a cinematic, stylish (and concise) movie that you can keep to yourself, or share with

the world. It's all about finding the perfect videographer to suit you and the feel of your wedding.
*(For the ultimate guide to the different types of wedding videography, turn to page 100.)*

If you decide you do need a videographer (and we hope you do), try to avoid asking a pal. Simply put, you won't get the same results as you would with a professional videographer. Plus, if you do ask a mate, they won't be able to fully enjoy the day as they'll be too busy working, so it's best to leave it to the professionals.

Your wedding day will go by so quickly and there are inevitably some parts that you'll forget or miss, so it'll be lovely to sit down and watch it all back with your new hubby or wifey. After all, when the excitement and glamour of your wedding day is over, all you'll have left (besides a beautiful new marriage) are your wedding photos and video. So make sure they're good 'uns.

# STYLES OF WEDDING VIDEOGRAPHY

### Cinematic

Filmed and edited to look like a movie, cinematic video really emphasises the emotion of the day. It might involve montages and special effects, like slow motion, and camera work is likely to feature more movement than traditional styles. Colours and contrast may be added later in order to give a more movie-like feel. Some shots will be set up and involve your videographer directing you, much like a real movie.

**Pros:** The result is a beautiful, feature film-like video.
**Cons:** Some shots may need to be set up, but it's totally worth it.

### Short form

Increasingly popular in wedding video, it's edited down to shorter clips of as little as 15 minutes and lends itself well to cinematic styles. It won't include the ceremony or speeches in full, just snippets

**Pros:** Makes for easier watching and sharing, as it's condensed.
**Cons:** Shorter than traditional videos.

### Journalistic

This is often referred to as documentary style and will involve the videographer capturing the events of the day in chronological order. Videos tend to be around 30 to 60 minutes and some videographers will include interviews with the wedding couple or guests and edit them in as soundbites. The videographer will hang back for the day, so as to not disrupt guests.

**Pros:** It's very unobtrusive.
**Cons:** Can be quite structured.

### Traditional

Traditional video covers your wedding from start to finish and could be as long as two hours. Minimal editing is required, so you'll get it back quite quickly.

**Pros:** Extensive coverage and a quick turnaround.
**Cons:** Not sharable online and too long to enjoy regularly. The service is no longer widely available in Ireland.

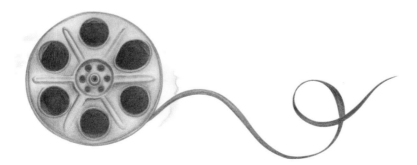

*Confetti loves...*
SELECTED SUPPLIERS

**WEDDING PHOTOGRAPHY & VIDEO**
WEDDINGPHOTOGRAPHYANDVIDEO.IE | TEL: 083 4545 588
INSTAGRAM: @ weddingphotographyandvideo.ie

# Photography notes

# Music

## LET'S DANCE

# Please Don't Stop The Music

Music, like love, forms the backbone of your wedding day. It sets the tone, tells a story and brings your guests on a journey. Choosing the various musical elements of your day is one of the most fun and creative parts, especially if music is your jam.

Whether you have a list of favourite songs that you always knew you'd incorporate, or you're starting from scratch scrolling through *Spotify* for inspiration, it's a real labour of love. And we guarantee your wedding playlist will get more than a few listens on the lead up – it really helps build the excitement.

Your ceremony is the first opportunity to inject your personalities into proceedings through your choice of performers and songs. Pick a style that will set the tone you're trying to achieve for the day. After that, spend time carefully choosing the songs that will form an integral part of proceedings. Your drinks reception is up next. Will you provide the venue with a playlist to set the mood? Or hire some musicians to entertain? Trad? A quartet? A Mariachi band on stilts? The options are endless.

After that, it's the all-important first dance – this is the big one. It should mean something to you as a couple, and also be something you can dance to. Throw all other rules out the window though – if Talking Heads' Psycho Killer is your song, go for it. The first dance's lesser-known little brother is the second dance; the song that really kicks evening proceedings off. Often, your band will have a winning track they typically start with, but if you have an up-tempo option in mind, let 'em know.

*All together now...*

# Types Of Ceremony Music

## Strings
A solo violinist, or if you're feeling flush, a string quartet, instantly creates an atmosphere of sophistication. Whether they're performing classical greats or classical adaptations of modern hits, your ceremony will be filled with soothing, romantic strains. This also works beautifully for drinks receptions, particularly at black tie affairs. String instruments work especially well in indoor spaces with harder surfaces, such as glass or marble, as the acoustics are perfect to amplify the sound. A church or grand foyer in a stately home is the perfect spot.

## Acoustic
If you're going for a more relaxed vibe, you can't beat an acoustic guitar. Alone or accompanied by a vocalist, it creates a welcoming, chilled mood. In larger venues, the sound can be amplified to fill the room, but if you're getting married on the grounds of your venue, it's a moveable feast that works anywhere.

## Choir
We can't think of anything more rousing than a gospel choir belting out *Oh Happy Day* as you walk down the aisle, as newlyweds. Choirs are an amazing addition to proceedings, whatever style you opt for. The good news is, you don't need a ten-strong troop. Often, four or five members is enough to give a full-bodied sound and party atmosphere.

## Classical
A classically trained soprano singing the right song is sure to touch your guests right in the feels. Add in the aforementioned strings and you have a recipe for Sobfest 2020.

## Crooner
A crooner is a Sinatra-style male vocalist who sings old school romantic ballads with plenty of added swagger. This works particularly well at drinks receptions, but can be a great addition to your ceremony too. Imagine walking up the aisle to the sounds of Sinatra's *It Had To Be You*, with your loved one waiting at the top. We're big fans of Sean Boland (*seanboland.ie*).

## Wind/brass instruments
Woodwinds like flute, clarinet and oboe are breathtakingly emotive at a wedding ceremony. We're thinking Ennio Morricone's *Gabriel's Oboe* during the signing of the registry – beautiful! Brass instruments such as the French horn and trumpet are super cool too. If you're having an outdoor ceremony, these louder instruments will work perfectly, as they will be able to project the perfect amount of sound without having to be amped up.

# POPULAR CEREMONY SONGS

Unless you're having a religious ceremony in which you're restricted to hymns, the world is your oyster then it comes to ceremony music. So make it emotional, make it uplifting and, above all, make it oh so you. Here are some popular options, from the classics right up to more modern choices...

## Processional
◊ *Bridal Chorus* by Wagner
◊ *Ave Maria* by Schubert
◊ *Clair de Lune* by Claude Debussy
◊ *Canon in D* by Johann Pachelbel
◊ *How Long Will I Love You?*, Ellie Goulding version
◊ *Songbird*, Eva Cassidy version
◊ *Hallelujah*, Jeff Buckley version
◊ *Higher Love*, James Vincent McMorrow version
◊ *Make You Feel My Love*, Adele version
◊ *Heavenly Day* by Patty Griffin
◊ *Evergreen* by Barbra Streisand
◊ *Hoppipolla* by Sigur Ros
◊ *Falling Slowly* by Glen Hansard and Marketa Irglova

## During the ceremony
◊ *Amazing Grace*, Judy Collins version
◊ *What a Wonderful World* by Louis Armstrong
◊ *The Voyage* by Christy Moore
◊ *The Power of Love*, Gabrielle Aplin version
◊ *Somewhere Only We Know* by Keane
◊ *Here Comes the Sun* by The Beatles
◊ *Kiss Me* by Ed Sheeran
◊ *The Only Exception* by Paramore

◊ *If I Ain't Got You* by Alicia Keys
◊ *Warm* by The Coronas
◊ *Don't Believe Me* by PictureHouse
◊ *His Eye is on The Sparrow*, Sister Act II version
◊ *A Rainy Night in Soho* by The Pogues
◊ *She Moves Through the Fair* (trad)

## Register/recessional
◊ *Signed, Sealed, Delivered (I'm Yours)* by Stevie Wonder
◊ *Nothing's Gonna Stop Us Now* by Starship
◊ *Walking on Sunshine* by Katrina & The Waves
◊ *One Day Like This* by Elbow
◊ *For Once in My Life* by Stevie Wonder
◊ *A Sky Full of Stars* by Coldplay
◊ *Love on Top* by Beyoncé
◊ *At Last* by Etta James
◊ *Beautiful Day* by U2
◊ *Greatest Day* by Take That
◊ *Oh Happy Day*, Sister Act II version
◊ *God Only Knows* by The Beach Boys
◊ *Heyday* by Mic Christopher
◊ *You Make My Dreams* by Hall & Oates
◊ *Bitter Sweet Symphony* by The Verve
◊ *Can't Take My Eyes Off You* by Frankie Valli

# DO I NEED A WEDDING BAND?

## Short answer? Yes.
One of the things that guests remember most after a wedding, is the music and, in particular, the band. Here's why...

## Let it go
Write down the type of music that fits your vision and wedding theme and the type of music you love to listen to. Next, throw that list in the bin - wedding music is a different beast altogether. A great wedding band knows how to entertain a very mixed crowd and will strike that elusive balance between modern classics, old school gems and full-blown party anthems (with a little dash of cheese thrown in for good measure). A mix of genres is essential and will keep everyone happy and, most importantly, dancing all night.

## Live action
Before you book, do your research. Narrow down a shortlist of bands you like and check out their YouTube or social media accounts. Ideally, go and see the band in action before you commit. Most wedding bands do regular showcases in pubs or clubs, so find out where they're playing that's local to you. Occasionally they'll get permission from another couple to let you pop into their reception to see them play. It's a great way to see how they interact with a crowd, how they dress for wedding gigs and the atmosphere they create. Finally, read reviews from previous couples on their websites.

## Is this thing on?
When choosing your band, consider the space they'll be playing in. Will that eight-piece set-up fit in your stretch tent? Will the two-piece be lost on the massive ballroom stage? Also, check with your reception venue to see if they have any restrictions on noise, number of musicians or amount of equipment and ensure they have sufficient power sources. A lot of larger bands have different packages with varying numbers of members, meaning you may be able to book your preferred band in a downsized version.

## Nigs!
Like any wedding vendor you hire, trust your band's expertise and don't over-direct them. You've booked them because you like what they do, so let them do it. You may, however, be able to make a special request for your first dance, or for them to include a song that means a lot to you during the night. Also, if there's anything on their setlist you absolutely hate, they may be happy to leave it out. You might be surprised at how well it goes down with your guests though, so try not to be too picky. But if you really can't stomach *Come On, Eileen* (shudder), ask if can be vetoed from the set.

# THINGS TO ASK YOUR WEDDING BAND BEFORE YOU BOOK

## The basics
1. Is our wedding date available?
2. Do you provide any additional services, such as a DJ?
3. Where can I read some testimonials?
4. Where can I see you perform?

## The music
5. Can we see your setlist?
6. What genres do you cover?
7. Can we submit a 'do not play' list?
8. Do you take breaks? If so, will there be music provided during the break?
9. Do you take requests?

## Pricing
10. What exactly is included in the cost?
11. Do you include travel fees in your cost or is that extra?

12. How much of a deposit do you need and when is it due?
13. What is your cancellation policy?
14. How far in advance do I need to book you?
15. Do you need any information from me before the wedding?

## Logistics
16. Does your equipment require any special electrical outlets?
17. Do you have a backup plan if one of the band members is sick?
18. Have you played at our venue before?
19. What do you usually wear to perform at weddings?
20. What time will you arrive to the venue?
21. How much time will you need for set-up, sound check and packing up?

BEFORE THE DAY I MET YOU
LIFE WAS SO UNKIND
But you're the key to
MY PEACE OF MIND

Aretha Franklin

# Popular First Dance Songs

Your first dance is a sweet moment, amongst the madness of your wedding day, where you share a romantic dance with your new hubby or wife, while all your friends and family watch in adoration. But what song do you choose? We've rounded up some of the most popular.

◇ *Thinking Out Loud* by Ed Sheeran
◇ *Better Together* by Jack Johnson
◇ *I'm Yours* by Jason Mraz
◇ *At Last* by Etta James
◇ *Ho Hey* by The Lumineers
◇ *All of Me* by John Legend
◇ *A Thousand Years* by Christina Perri
◇ *Your Song* by Elton John
◇ *Everything* by Michael Bublé
◇ *Can't Help Falling in Love* by Elvis Presley
◇ *Let's Stay Together* by Al Green
◇ *You Are the Best Thing* by Ray LaMontagne
◇ *Tiny Dancer* by Elton John
◇ *Say You Won't Let Go* by James Arthur
◇ *Wonderful Tonight* by Eric Clapton
◇ *Dancing in the Moonlight*, Van Morrison version
◇ *Toothpaste Kisses* by The Maccabees
◇ *It Had To Be You* by Frank Sinatra
◇ *Close To You* by The Carpenters
◇ *Rule The World* by Take That
◇ *For Once In My Life* by Stevie Wonder
◇ *Never Too Much* by Luther Vandross

# Do I Need A DJ?

Weddings cost serious cash and we're all looking to cut corners where we can, so it's tempting to decide that an iPhone on shuffle with your favourite songs will do the job of a professional DJ. But, with music being pivotal in how a party goes, we think it's worth every cent...

**Please don't stop the music...**
The fear of technical difficulties disrupting proceedings is reason enough to have a professional look after the tunes. Nothing will kill a party quicker than the music skipping or stopping. You don't want to end up scrambling around looking for a solution when you're meant to be doing *The Harlem Shake*. With a DJ in place, you know you're all set.

**Crowd pleaser**
Great wedding music isn't necessarily a list of your favourite tunes. Much like your band, your DJ has probably performed at hundreds of weddings and knows the perfect mix of old and new, cool and absolute cheese, to keep everyone dancing. Let them do their thing and your dance floor will be full all night.

**I'm with the band**
Many wedding bands offer a DJ service as part of the package and this can work out to be very reasonable. Chat to them and see what your options are.

**Hey Mr. DJ**
Even though it's not live music, you can't beat the atmosphere created by a DJ. The excitement when they play a song everyone loves or drop and cheesy tune you haven't heard in years, is irreplaceable.

*"Nothing will kill a party quicker than the music skipping or stopping"*

# THINGS TO ASK YOUR DJ

1. Are you available on our wedding date?

2. Do you provide a written contract?

3. Is there a deposit required? If so, how far in advance do we need to provide it?

4. Will you take my playlist or 'do not play' list into account?

5. Do you mix tracks or play back-to-back?

6. Will you require a break?

7. Do you take guest requests?

8. Will you act as emcee for the likes of cutting the cake and toasts, etc.? If so, is there an extra fee for this?

9. Have you DJ'd at our reception venue before?

10. What's your cancellation policy?

11. What happens if you're sick on the day, do you have a backup? If so, can you provide us with information about them?

12. Do you offer any other services, such as special effects or lighting displays?

13. Do you play all genres or only specific ones?

14. How long does your set last for? If we would like you to play longer, is that possible and how much extra do you charge?

15. Are you DJ'ing anywhere near me soon, so I could go see you?

16. What do you typically wear to DJ weddings?

# TOP TIPS

**All Night Long**

If you want your party to go late, consider arranging some entertainment for the 'after party'. Hiring a musician or group to perform in the residents' bar (with the venue's permission, of course) keeps the party gong longer. Add on the requisite sing-song at the end and you're well into tomorrow.

**Rock it out**

Don't feel you need to match your music style to your venue. Just because you're getting married in a grand, stately home, doesn't mean you have to have a string quartet and stuffy jazz band in tuxes. You book that fun 80s pop band, girl! The more neon sweatbands, the better.

# Entertainment

## IT'S PARTY TIME

# Where The Party At?

Next to the actual getting married bit, entertainment is arguably the second-most important part of your wedding day. After all, it's a celebration and should feel like one big old party. And the fun doesn't just start at your reception, there are lots of creative ways of introducing entertaining elements into your day, ensuring that you and your guests have the best day ever. This chapter aims to spark your imagination and inspire ideas for just that.

The flow of your day defines the experience for everyone there, so remember, you don't have to be a slave to the traditional timeline. If you want to have your speeches during your drinks reception, go for it. Or if a casual BBQ or buffet is more your vibe than a sit-down meal, do it. Our best advice is to avoid too much downtime. Drinks receptions are great, but tummies will start to rumble and small talk will run out, so make sure to keep things moving and your pals, entertained. *We have lots of fun ideas for this on page 114.*

When the after party kicks off, a full dancefloor is obviously preferable but it's a mistake to police people's fun too much. Some of the best craic at weddings is had over tipsy chats in the gardens or giddy games at the bar. Let your guests mix and mingle as they please and trust that they're having a great time, wherever they are.

The ideal scenario is feeling like a guest at your own wedding. You've spent months planning those entertaining extras, so make sure to enjoy them yourself. Get stuck in to that photobooth and play some silly lawn games with your family and faves - it's quality time you'll remember forever.

*Let's party!*

# Entertaining Extras

You've probably agonised over the shade of your ties or the perfect flavours for your cake, but when it comes down to it, your guests will remember the experience more than the details. If you want the fun to stand out over the favours, an entertaining extra will never go amiss...

### Photobooths/DIY selfie stations
The photobooth trend is one guests will never get sick of. When everyone's all dolled up, they're only delighted to have an opportunity for a photo, and it's nice to be able to take your snaps home at the end of the night. Guests love nothing more than a wig, waving some cutesy props and striking a pose. A video booth is another fun option, as it captures all the real-time action.

### Lawn games
Let your inner child shine by setting up garden games to entertain guests during the drinks reception. Giant Jenga or Connect Four, boules, croquet, ring toss, or even just a few hurls and sliotars should do the trick. Not having an outdoor part? Classic board games are always a hit.

### Cocktail station
We love a good sweet cart but a custom cocktail bar adds something a little different to your day. Set up a DIY station, with ingredients, garnishes and instructions on how to make your favourites, or hire a mixologist to whip up a custom cocktail you've designed. It's a nice alternative to a Champagne reception if Champagne/Prosecco aren't your jam.

### Singing waiters
If you're looking to surprise your guests as they tuck into their meal, singing waiters are the way to go. Dressed as waiting staff, these guys blend in until dinner time, when they break into song and dance, usually serving up Broadway and West End hits, offering guests a show-stopping performance as they tuck into their trio of desserts. You can also hire a singing firefighter, who'll burst into song after what your guests think is a fire drill announcement - gas!

### Caricaturist
Hire a caricaturist or illustrator to sketch guests on the day. They can add your monogram or wedding date and, boom, you have a lovely keepsake that can double up as a favour for your wedding guests.

## Comedians and magicians

These are an excellent way to get your guests into the party spirit during the drinks reception or as dinner winds down. Comedians will amuse your guests with impersonations and skits, while magicians will use a mix of tricks, mind-reading and illusions. Both will get your guests mingling and laughing along.

## Sparklers

After dinner, before the dancing gets going, sparklers provide an ideal photo opportunity that gets all your guests involved. Check in advance with your venue where is safest to light them, and make sure to have multiple lighters on hand so they all get lit at once. You can use them to 'write' words in the night sky or run through a tunnel of sparklers created by your guests, to provide a real wow moment at the end of the evening.

## Silent disco

Think your friends and family know how to have a good time? A silent disco will likely be right up their street. The atmosphere created during a silent disco, where everyone is listening to different playlists through headphones, all at once, can't be matched. One for after everyone's had a few drinks, guest will embrace the funny-fitting headphones and find the tunes to suit the party they want to have. Win-win for all. Also, if there are noise restrictions at your venue, this is your loophole.

## Resident's bar

There ain't no party like an Irish wedding party, and you can almost be guaranteed that, as the night goes on, your guests will be looking towards the resident's bar for a traditional sing-song to end the night, or start the morning, as is often the case. If you have pals who play the guitar, ask them to throw them in the boot just in case, and if you're in luck, the bar may even have a piano ready and waiting for you. "Everybody! Sing us a song, you're the piano man..."

# DAY TWO ENTERTAINMENT

### Fun ideas for rollover festivities

The second day of a weekend wedding is often just as much fun, and the good news for couples is that you'll be a whole heap less stressed and nervous than you potentially were the day before. It's an amazing chance to hang out with your pals and family, absorb all the love and chat about the events of your wedding day. They're mostly very relaxed affairs involving a boozy brunch or BBQ and the odd sing-song, but why not inject some fun and games into proceedings, with one of these activities? They take a bit of organising, but we all have a mate who would love the idea of playing games master. Delegate the job and take part in the fun yourselves. **Warning:** You may come up against some resistance from hungover heads, but with a bit of encouragement, everyone will have a great time and it will really help blow the cobwebs off.

### Treasure hunt with a twist

This works particularly well for summer weddings at venues with ample grounds. Instead of the traditional treasure hunt, design a series of challenges for teams to carry out. Assign a photo taker on each team to take phone snaps of their team completing each task. Some of our favourites are squeezing your team into the smallest space possible (a phone box or bath tub works well), a member of your team pretending to propose to a random stranger or everyone on the team switching clothes. The first team back at base after completing every task, with photo evidence of each one, wins the glory and perhaps a round of drinks. Trust us, this will go down a treat and create some of the funniest photos from the whole wedding weekend.

### Themed table quiz

If the weather isn't on your side, a good old fashioned table quiz will provide endless entertainment. Create rounds about you as a couple and don't be afraid to poke fun at yourselves. Make it personal to your guests and families too, by including questions on their specialist subjects. If you're big GAA fans, or a very musical family, make that a part of it. Competitive streaks will show, but many laughs will be had.

### Adult sports day

Go old school with sack races, hurdles and egg and spoon races on the grass. Make sure to let your guests know in advance, so they can pack some trackies and trainers. Pick up some inexpensive medals and trophies on ebay or Amazon and have a tongue-in-cheek medal ceremony for the winners. Bonus points if you build a DIY podium for this – the photos will be pretty gas.

# ENTERTAINING THE CHILDREN

Having a kid-friendly shindig? The little 'uns will love these fun additions.

### Let's bounce
What could be more fun than a bouncing castle for the kids to hop around in before dinner? Be sure to clear this one with your venue first, of course. After that, the only struggle will be to try keep the big kids (i.e. adults) off it. Good luck with that.

### Balloon bonanza
Why not hire in a balloon maker to keep the little ones occupied? They'll knock a couple hours of fun out of having their favourite animals transformed into super cool balloon pals.

### Lawn games
If your reception venue has decent gardens, and you happen to be lucky with the weather, lay out some old-fashioned lawn games for the younger guests.

### Rainy day fun
If it's a rainy day (we promise, you won't care), set up a boardgame area indoors. This is a great option for both younger and older kids.

### Art attack
Kids love arts and crafts, so set up an area with dry craft supplies such as feathers, stickers, pipe cleaners, colourful paper and some crafty tools. Avoid paints and glue to keep them clean and parents, happy.

### Colour by numbers
Turn the kids' menus into fun colouring sheets, to prevent them getting restless while they're waiting for dinner. Maybe offer a little prize for the best colouring, as an incentive/peace-keeping initiative.

### Photo challenge
Disposable cameras and a list of shots to take will keep kids occupied during your drinks reception. Task them with snapping things like the youngest guest, the flowers or the venue's dog and they'll have great fun rising to the challenge.

### Cheers, big ears!
The adults will get to raise a glass, so the kids should too. How about a milk and cookies toast? They'll feel included and think it's great craic.

### Babysitters club
Consider hiring a babysitter to make sure that the kid-based activities go off without a hitch and there are no sticky fingermarks on the cake. This means that you (and their parents) can relax knowing the situation's under control.

YOU MAKE THE MOON
OUR MIRROR BALL.
The streets, an empty stage.
THE CITY'S SIRENS, VIOLINS.
EVERYTHING HAS CHANGED

Elbow

# Making Your Speeches Fun

Your wedding speeches don't have to be (nor should they be) long and drawn out. We all know this, right? But what if you presume they'll be done in half an hour, only to find yourself rolling your eyes at your other half as it creeps into hour two, including countless embarrassing anecdotes, a PowerPoint presentation and two songs? You've planned every other aspect of the day to a T, so you should have an input into speech time too. Encourage speakers to keep them concise and as casual as they're comfortable with. Chances are, they'll be relieved that you only want them to speak for five or ten minutes each. That way guests aren't eyeing up their escape route to the bar and you'll have a much better handle on the timings of the evening, which is always essential.

Feel free to veto certain subjects too, in case your best man thinks it's only gas to refer to that time you guys broke up for a summer and they partied it up in Ibiza. A gentle jibe is okay, but a full-on roast is not appropriate for the day that's in it, so choose your speakers wisely and warn any wildcards that one will not be amused, should they go off-piste.

Speeches are traditionally carried out after the meal, but because speakers are often full of nerves, and therefore potentially unable to enjoy their dinner, before the meal is a more popular choice these days. Between courses is another good option, but this can cause problems for serving staff, so make sure your venue knows the schedule and can time things accordingly.

Of course, if the traditional speech set-up isn't rocking your world, mix it up and design your own. Directly after the ceremony while everyone's having a drink is always fun too. Your day, your way and all that good stuff.

Traditionally speaking, only the men in your bridal party get up to say a few words but we're not about that life. Brides, mothers of both, chief bridesmaids – let's hear it from you.

*"If the traditional speech set-up isn't rocking your world, mix it up and design your own"*

# TOP TIPS

**Cheers!**
Everyone loves a little DIY. Instead of serving a signature cocktail, invite guests to design their own by setting up a 'Pimp my Prosecco' station or self-service gin bar with plenty of garnishes to choose from. Pimm's is also a great option for a summer bash and always goes down a treat. Don't forget a non-alcoholic version for teetotalers and drivers.

**Don't stress**
Whilst avoiding long lulls is advisable, don't worry too much about entertaining your guests for every single second of the day. Once they're fed and watered, they'll make their own fun. Stationary elements like selfie stations and photo walls are great ice-breakers and talking points that don't cost the earth or require manpower on the day itself.

# Entertainment notes

# Entertainment notes

# The Guest List

## PICKING YOUR PARTY PEOPLE

# Where Are Your Friends Tonight?

People make a party, everything else is just window dressing. When you're dancing, sweaty-faced, in a circle with your best girls, or doing shots at the bar with your Dad, all the months of meticulous planning will have been worth every second and, all at once, mean absolutely nothing. Being surrounded by the ones you love and who love you back, ferociously, will be all that matters. A wedding is an incomparable love bubble, full to bursting point with raw emotion and togetherness.

Admittedly, some of the planning that goes into making sure all your faves are there can be some of the most stressful. RSVP chasing and seating plan design are the things we hear couples bemoan the most. In this chapter we aim to break it all down, hopefully making them into less daunting tasks in the process.

The guest list is also the main area that's likely to cause friction. Family members who don't get an invitation, pals put out by not getting a plus one and parents giving out about their little ones not being invited are all too common. Mentally prepare yourself for this from the get-go so that, when it happens, you're not too thrown. Remind yourself that it was inevitable and that you can't (nor should you try to) please all of the people, all of the time.

When the day comes around (and it'll come around quicker than you can fathom), it will all have blown over and you'll be marrying your beau with your gang all around you.

*You've got this!*

# Your seat awaits

**Table 1**
Laura C
Aimee
Aoife
Aisling

**Table 2**
Karen
Neil
Paul G
Amanda

**Table 3**
Carol
Tanya
Aine
Layla

**Table 4**
Colm
Sharon
Anna
Phil

**Table 5**
Bill
Fiona
Richard
Jane

**Table 6**
Alan
Paula
Brendan
Caron

**Table 7**
Laura M
Greg
Paul M
Ali

**Table 8**
Kirstie
Ismael
Lisa
Emmett

**Table 9**
Moya
Anuette
Louise
Juliette

**Table 10**
Vicky
Paul
Pamela
Matt

**Table 11**
Marie
Johnny
Margaret
Elaine

**Table 12**
John
Caitriona
Hannah
Sean

# Should We Invite Them?

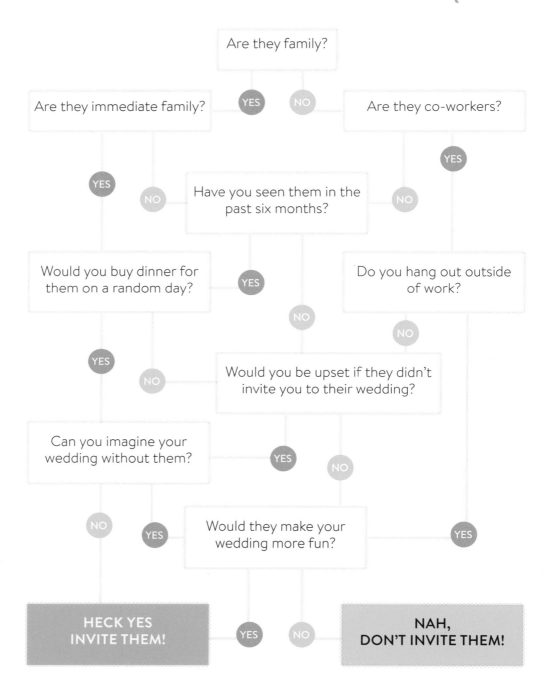

Are they family?
- YES → Are they immediate family?
- NO → Are they co-workers?

**Are they immediate family?**
- YES → HECK YES INVITE THEM!
- NO → Have you seen them in the past six months?

**Are they co-workers?**
- YES → Do you hang out outside of work?
- NO → Have you seen them in the past six months?

**Have you seen them in the past six months?**
- YES → Would you buy dinner for them on a random day?
- NO → Would you be upset if they didn't invite you to their wedding?

**Would you buy dinner for them on a random day?**
- YES → HECK YES INVITE THEM!
- NO → Would you be upset if they didn't invite you to their wedding?

**Do you hang out outside of work?**
- NO → Would you be upset if they didn't invite you to their wedding?

**Would you be upset if they didn't invite you to their wedding?**
- YES → Can you imagine your wedding without them?
- NO → Would they make your wedding more fun?

**Can you imagine your wedding without them?**
- YES → Would they make your wedding more fun?
- NO → HECK YES INVITE THEM!

**Would they make your wedding more fun?**
- YES → HECK YES INVITE THEM!
- NO → NAH, DON'T INVITE THEM!

**HECK YES INVITE THEM!**

**NAH, DON'T INVITE THEM!**

# DO I REALLY HAVE TO INVITE...

## My boss?
This very much depends on your relationship with them. If you get on well and they've met your fiancé, it's polite to invite them, even if you're not exactly besties outside work.

## My parent's friends?
If they're paying for some or all of your wedding, it's only fair to let them invite as many guests as they like. Either way, it's sound to let them bring some pals. You'll run into trouble if your venue is tight on space, so sit down and chat about what's a reasonable number.

## My colleagues?
You'll probably invite a small number of your closest colleagues, but if you tend to keep your work and personal life very separate, you're certainly not obliged to. If you're super-close to your work gang, but don't have space for everyone and their other halves, ask them if they mind coming together, without dates, and save a table for them.

## My younger cousins?
In Irish families, cousin numbers tend to run high and you probably can't invite them all. If you have a big family, establish a cut-off point, such as only those who are over 21 or a limit of two 'kids' from each family.

## The priest/vicar?
This is up to you but, in some parishes, it's very much the done thing. Whether you're besties with your priest or not, he will always be the man who married you, so it might be nice to have him celebrate with you afterwards.

## Someone I haven't seen in years?
If your numbers are tight, the obvious course is to invite your nearest and dearest first, without feeling pressure to return the favour to that old school friend whose wedding you attended a couple of years ago. Maybe drop them an email letting them know that yours is a much more intimate shindig, but you'd love to see them at the afters or second-day celebrations.

*"If you're super close to your work gang, but don't have space for everyone and their other halves, ask them to come together without dates"*

# Kids Or No Kids?

## The question that divides a nation

Deciding whether or not to have children at your wedding is a big call to make. You'll encounter polarised opinions, with some parents excited for a night without their little ones and others, put out at having to leave them. Prepare yourself to hear, "I know you're not having kids, but can mine go? She's so good!" It will happen. Our best advice is to go with your gut and stick with it. Whatever you decide, don't make exceptions, or there will be trouble! Here are the pros and cons of inviting them along.

### Pros

◇ You'll avoid the awkwardness of telling guests they can't bring their little darlings to your day.

◇ Including flowergirls or pageboys in your ceremony is super sweet.

◇ It makes attending your wedding doable for parents who don't have anyone to mind the troop.

◇ Kids are gas and they'll add playfulness to your day. Arrange some entertainment to keep them occupied during the reception. *For more on this, see page 117.*

◇ Extending an invite to kids is a great way to let your wedding double as a family reunion. It's a brilliant opportunity to see far-flung nieces, nephews or cousins you may not have seen since they were born. Lovely!

### Cons

◇ Expecting multiple children to remain silent during your ceremony is ambitious at best. If you're inviting kids, you better make friends with the fact that a baby will probably cry during your vows. You'll either think this is a big deal or you won't.

◇ Add new surroundings and sugar to a group of kids and you have yourself a big old recipe for hyperactivity. If you love to see children letting loose and just being kids, you won't mind this at all. But if the idea of a gang of kiddies running rampant around your reception upsets you, maybe it's a no from you.

◇ Keep in mind that kids meals are not free, so it'll cost you more to have them there.

◇ If space at your venue is limited, you might have to forgo potential adult guests to make space for other guests' kids.

# The Great
## PLUS ONE DEBATE

Budget and space limitations may not allow you to invite everyone you'd like, plus their partner. However, proper etiquette dictates that guests are a package deal, so what's a couple to do?

### The rules
Married pals, those cohabiting and couples with a long-standing commitment to one another should always be invited together – anything else could be seen as a snub.

### The grey areas
Guests in new relationships, that may not even have existed when the Save The Dates went out, won't necessarily expect a plus one. But, if you can swing it, we're sure they'll be delighted. Make a decision to draw the line somewhere, perhaps only including couples who have been together for at least six months.

### Exceptions
If you're inviting a gaggle of younger cousins, we're sure they'll understand if you don't have room for all of their boyfriends and girlfriends and will be happy to attend as a family group instead. It's also okay to invite a table of work pals, or the girls from your football team, to come together without their other halves.

### What about people you don't like?
If you couldn't live without a certain friend being there, but despise their partner, it's never okay to leave them out. Suck it up – you probably won't see them much anyway.

YOU'RE THE
chocolate
AT THE END OF MY
Cornetto

Bell XI

# Invitation Etiquette & Timelines

### Engagement party

Getting engaged is so exciting and you're forgiven for wanting the world and its granny to celebrate with you, but beware of the engagement party trap! Etiquette states that you only invite future wedding guests to your engagement drinks, so don't get carried away. Not inviting them to the main event after they've partied hard with you and maybe even bought you a gift, might be mega awkward. If you have no idea of your numbers yet, make your engagement drinks a nearest and dearest affair.

### Save The Dates

These go out anywhere between a year and three months before the wedding. If you have guests traveling from abroad or if you're having a destination wedding, send them as early as possible. This is also a great way of letting certain people know that they're not invited – that presumptuous cousin who booked her accommodation six months in advance, presuming she'll get the nod, will soon get the hint.

### Invitations

Traditionally, invitations go out about six to eight weeks before the wedding, which gives guests plenty of time to finalise any travel or accommodation plans. If it's a destination wedding, send them much earlier (at least four months before) as your guests will need to book flights and get time off work. (*For everything you need to include with your invitations, see our guide on page 135.*)

### RSVP

The ideal RSVP deadline is roughly two to three weeks before the wedding. This will allow you plenty of time to get final numbers to your venue or caterers (usually one week before the wedding), and to get cracking on your seating chart.

"*Getting engaged is so exciting and you're forgiven for wanting the world and its granny to celebrate with you*"

# Invitation Wording

Your wedding invitations don't just impart information, they give your guests the first taster of your wedding style. Preparing and sending them is a big job, but it's an exciting time that often helps things start to feel very real. Getting the wording right is important, so follow our handy guide.

## Host line

This first line should list who will be hosting the wedding. Traditionally, a bride's parents footed the bill, so they would naturally be listed as the host. If both families are contributing, your host line could simply read 'together with their families'. Or, if you're paying for the wedding yourselves, you can omit the host line entirely, and go straight to the names line.

## Names

This part is pretty self-explanatory – the couple's names go on this line. But, whose name goes first? Traditionally, it's a bride's name. If there are two brides or two grooms, flip a coin or go with whatever looks best visually on the page – your designer will advise.

## Invitation line

This is quite literally where you invite your guests to your wedding. This line will follow the name of the couple and usually reads something like 'invite you to join them as they celebrate their marriage' or 'request the honour of the company of...'. This is followed by the invitee's name.

## Ceremony information

This is where you should include the time, date and location of your ceremony. Keep it simple – you don't necessarily need to include the full address, unless it's not particularly easy to find.

## Reception information

Something like 'dinner and dancing to follow' at your reception venue. There's no need to put a time on this, as it's assumed as soon as the ceremony is over, that guests will make their way to the reception. If you're not serving a full meal, it's advisable to specify this here – for example, 'light bites and cocktails to follow'.

## Dress code (optional)

If there's a dress code, let the guests know here.

TOGETHER WITH
THEIR FAMILIES

HEATHER CONDREN

DOUG WHELAN

INVITE YOU TO JOIN THEM AT THE
CELEBRATION OF THEIR MARRIAGE

FRIDAY 14TH OF APRIL
TWO THOUSAND AND SEVENTEEN
AT TWO IN THE AFTERNOON

MOUNT DRUID
CASTLETOWN GEOGHEGAN,
CO. WESTMEATH

DINNER AND DANCING
TO FOLLOW

Host line

Names

Invitation
line

Ceremony
information

Reception
information

Dress code
optional

# WHY IS NO ONE RSVP'ING TO MY WEDDING?

So you've sent your invitations and are now excitedly awaiting the influx of positive responses. So, eh, where are they? A number of super-organised guests will reply almost straight away, but they may be in the minority. Give yourself the best chance with these handy tips...

### Step one: Keep it simple

Include a self-addressed envelope for your RSVP card, making it easier for guests to fill it out and send it back right away, before it gets lost in that 'drawer of shame' we all have in our kitchens. Make sure the deadline date is clearly printed on the card, so your guests are well aware of the cut-off point.

### Step two: Gentle reminder

If it's getting increasingly close to the cut-off point, it's totally acceptable to give remaining guests a gentle nudge. Depending on how well you know them, send them a quick text or email to remind them to RSVP, as you need to know final numbers for your reception. If it's a friend of your parents or an older relative, let your folks do the leg-work for you. They probably know them better, and you haven't got all day to be chasing guests. Delegation is key, especially so close to the wedding.

### Step three: Final push

If the wedding is a fortnight away and you're still waiting to hear back from someone, it's time to up your game. Make a list of everyone you've yet to hear back from and pick up the phone. They're likely to let you know right away if they're attending or not, having simply forgotten to respond. Don't get mad – we've all been that soldier.

# WHAT TO INCLUDE WITH YOUR INVITATIONS

## 1. Wedding Invitation
The most important bit, this will detail the date, time and your ceremony and reception venues.

## 2. RSVP card
The response card allows guests to indicate whether they can make it or not. Top tip: Number each card and create a spreadsheet with your guests names and their corresponding numbers so that if a card returns with an illegible name, you can easily find out who it belongs to.

## 3. Dress code
This will usually be written on the main invitation, but if you have to expand on it for any reason, you'll need to include extra information. For example, if you're having a rustic barn wedding or a ceremony on a cliff side, you may need to advise on appropriate footwear.

## 4. Directions
If your venue is in a rural or obscure part of the country, or indeed, if it's a destination wedding, you should include a directions card. You can only rely on Google Maps for so long, and your guests may run out of coverage or phone battery, so it's handy if they have physical directions to hand.

## 5. Accommodation
Depending on how many rooms your venue offers, you may need to advise guests about extra accommodation options. Include details of nearby B&Bs and hotels. This will be especially helpful for any guests traveling from out-of-town.

## 6. Taxi numbers
If your guests aren't staying at your reception venue, provide them with a card of local taxi numbers, so they can ring ahead and pre-book their travel to and from your venue.

## 7. Day two information
If you're having a 'day two' celebration, provide your guests with details of the location and timings.

## 8. Gift list info
If you're having a gift list, you may choose to include this. Alternatively, share it with guests who request it.

# WEDDING WEBSITES

Wedding websites are certainly not a necessity, but they can serve as a very useful tool for your guests, particularly if you're marrying abroad or a far-flung part of the country

Include the following information so guests know what's what, long after they've misplaced that paper invitation you agonised over...

## Dates and timings
◇ The travel and accommodation options available
◇ Dress code information
◇ Details of activities happening over the weekend
◇ A link to your gift registry, if you're having one
◇ Locality information, for destination weddings
◇ Your social media hashtag (if you're having one)
◇ Or details of your 'unplugged' rule

Just as your wedding invitations announce your theme, your wedding website can do the same. It will make your nearest and dearest feel involved and excited for the big event. Avoid nosy Normans, wedding crashers and dreaded copycat brides by password-protecting your site, so that only your guests have access.

## Appy planning
The good news is, you don't have to employ a developer and build a website from scratch, as there are plenty of online platforms out there. Some are free and some more premium ones require a monthly or yearly fee. For this you'll get a wider choice of themes and extra features. Check some of these out:

1. The Knot, *theknot.com* (Free)

2. Wedding Wire, *weddingwire.com* (Free)

3. Joy, *withjoy.com* (Free)

4. SquareSpace, *squarespace.com* (Free trial/€11 per month)

5. Appy Couple, *appycouple.com* (€50/€150 one-time fee)

6. Riley & Grey, *rileygrey.com* (€30 per month/€205 per year)

# Seating Plan 101

Designing your seating plan can be stressful but it doesn't have to be. Read on for our simple breakdown, then take a few deep breaths. You can do this!

### First things first

Once you've decided on final numbers, find out how many tables you can fit into your reception room, the number of guests each table can accommodate, and whether tables are round or long. You're then ready to lay out your seating plan. There are a few ways to do this. You could go old school by drawing out a floor plan and placing sticky tabs with guests' names on them at each table, or opt for one of the many seating plan apps available online.

### Top table?

Traditionally, the couple and hosts sit at a long top table, ensuring they don't have their back to guests, but there's no rule to say you have to do this. Many couples opt to sit at a round table in the centre of the room with their parents and bridal party. Another fun idea is to sit your parents and siblings with you and your bridal party and their other halves at the next table. It's your wedding, so do it your way.

### The basics

Obvious groups such as your colleagues or college gang are easy to place, but what about the individual couples and singletons? The rule of thumb is to sit like-minded folks together for the best chance of good craic. When it comes to singletons, few people like the mortification of being obviously sat beside another single person at a wedding, so be subtle about that stuff.

### Positioning

Place exes or anyone who doesn't see eye to eye as far apart in the room as you can, but if it's not possible, don't fret about it too much. Everyone will make the effort for your wedding day. Elderly, infirm guests or guests with disabilities should be given the most accessible seat possible. And place the party crowd near the dancefloor for a lively atmosphere. See? Easy!

# Guest List notes

# Beauty

### PUTTING THE 'RIDE' IN BRIDE

# Line of Beauty

Let's face it, everyone wants to be a ridey bridey or a gorgeous groom. This is a chapter where it would be easy for us to lay on some serious pressure, with a never-ending list of ways in which you have to change yourself before your wedding. But that's just not our bag. In fact, if you put into practice every single aspect of wedding beauty we're about to cover here, you'd be unrecognisable when you meet your betrothed at the top of the aisle. So choose the bits that matter to you. This isn't about overhauling your appearance, it's about allowing yourself the indulgence of taking care of yourself, so that you look and feel your very best when your eyes ping open on the morning of your wedding. This is your year and, hey, you're worth it.

Consider the areas you'd like to work on, whether that's achieving glowing skin or improving your hair's condition, and put a plan in place and get to work as early as possible. Now's the time to bow to the experience of the pros, particularly in the areas of skincare and hair. Feeling around in the dark, trying out every conceivable product you can, may not bear the fruit you're hoping for. Targeted, educated advice is the name of the game and will set you on the right path.

Bridal beauty can feel like a mountain to climb, especially for anyone who isn't particularly interested in beauty 'in real life'. We'd urge you to look at the process as fun pampering, instead of fixing. Enjoy those facials and laugh off the epic failure of a spray tan trial that just didn't work out. And above all else, remember that when the day rocks around, the most beautiful part of you will be the whopper smile you couldn't wipe off your face if you tried.

*Happy pampering!*

# 12-MONTH
# Beauty Countdown

## 12 MONTHS TO GO:
- ◇ Have a consultation with a facialist or dermatologist
- ◇ Start your at-home skincare regime
- ◇ Begin taking any recommended supplements
- ◇ Visit your dentist if you're having teeth whitening or braces
- ◇ Make a 12-month plan for luscious locks with your hair stylist
- ◇ Start growing out your brows and get a patch test for tinting
- ◇ Begin laser hair removal

## 9 MONTHS TO GO:
- ◇ Make a conscious effort to start drinking more water
- ◇ Introduce good fats and reduce sugar intake for skin health
- ◇ Commence a workout regime, if desired

## 6 MONTHS TO GO:
- ◇ If you're considering a Botox treatment, visit your clinic now

## 3 MONTHS TO GO:
- ◇ Begin trials for hair, makeup and spray tan
- ◇ Have your first lash extension trial
- ◇ Start regular manicures now

## 1 MONTH TO GO:
- ◇ Have a massage – it's going to be a big month!
- ◇ Have any final hair and makeup trials now
- ◇ Get in some light exercise, if you can

## 2 WEEKS TO GO:

◇ Have your final teeth whitening appointment
◇ Let your skin breathe as much as possible, only wearing makeup when necessary
◇ Practice mindfulness and calm

## 1 WEEK TO GO:

◇ Get your final hair colour and treatments
◇ Visit your lash extention expert for a top up
◇ Take a long walk to clear your mind

## 3 DAYS TO GO:

◇ Have your brows done
◇ Take a long bath!

## 2 DAYS TO GO:

◇ Take care of any waxing
◇ Pop a hair masque in overnight

## THE DAY BEFORE

◇ Have your wedding nails done
◇ Get a spray tan
◇ Chill out with your bridal party
◇ Breathe!

## ON THE DAY

◇ Leave plenty of time for hair and makeup
◇ Sip a glass of bubbly and enjoy – IT'S TIME!

# Wed-Prep Skincare

Pre-wedding skincare is a marathon, not a last-minute sprint. So start early and make sure you have the right trainer.

## Ask an expert

While recommendations from friends and beauty blogs are fantastic in certain instances, don't fall into the trap of spending a fortune on products that don't suit your skin and therefore won't be effective. If you really want to up your skin game for your wedding, seeking advice from a professional - whether that's a dermatologist or a highly trained facialist - is key. They'll assess your skin type, determine what your challenges are and make a targeted plan of action that will actually work.

## The masterplan

Your skincare regime will more than likely involve the following:
Facials: One every six or eight weeks, plus a final session on the week of your wedding. They should be hydrating, detoxifying, peeling and plumping, all of which combined will achieve great results.

The RIGHT products: Getting these right early is vital. Playing around with new skincare products a few weeks before your wedding is not advisable. Your skin practitioner will tell you what's best to use, but here are some useful points to remember...

1. You can use multiple brands
2. Spend the most on products with good active ingredients like hyaluronic acid
3. What works for your best friend, or even your sister, might not work for you
4. Bear in mind your skin type (i.e. normal, combination, dry, oily) and your skin condition (i.e. dehydrated, sun damaged, acne, pigmentation)
5. You don't need to spend a huge amount of money on products to achieve a good result

## Going deeper

If you have the budget and want to delve a little deeper with issues like pigmentation, broken capillaries and deep set lines, there are a lot of great options out there that are very effective.

Peels: These are carried out by a trained professional and use acids such as glycolic, lactic and citric to resurface and retexturise the skin

IPL: A laser treatment which targets redness, pigmentation and broken veins and capillaries

Botox: Lots of brides opt for a bit of 'Baby Botox' to refresh their complexion and even out lines they don't like. *More on this on page 153.*

# FEEDING THE SKIN FROM WITHIN

Jennifer Rock, aka The Skin Nerd (*theskinnerd.com*), taught us it's about more than what we put ON our skin...

## Stress

If you're stressed out, your skin is feeling it too. It's easier said than done, but trying to decompress can keep your skin balanced. Jennifer says: "Stress plays havoc with the skin, changing it's healing ability, nourishment capacity and oil levels."

## Diet

Too much sugar in your diet dehydrates, saps your skin of plumpness, and can lead to breakouts. Jennifer says: "Eat green and orange foods. Why? Because greens (mojitos do not count!) have an anti-inflammatory effect on many irritants. Broccoli, green peppers, orange peppers, sweet potatoes – eat the rainbow. The essential fatty acids in nuts, seeds and fish oils will plump the skin like no moisturiser."

## Tiredness

Not getting enough sleep can lead to dark circles, and a general grey pallor that is difficult to fix with makeup.

Try to regulate your sleep pattern where possible.

## Vitamin deficiency

A deficiency in certain vitamins can mean your skin isn't feeling or looking its best. Talk to your dermatologist or a facialist about what they'd recommend for you. Jennifer says: "Take vitamin C for your skins clarity and general body functioning."

## Water

Drink it. Lots of it!

## HELP ME, SKIN NERD! I HAVE A WEDDING WEEK BREAKOUT!

Jennifer says: "SOS must-haves for wedding week include a salicylic acid-based mask or lotion to put on any spot that dares to appear. I like *Acne Out* from Biofresh, a hydrating hyaluronic mask like *YonKa Masque No1*, and *IMAGE Iluma Powder* mixed into any cleanser, to buff and brighten."

*"Too much sugar dehydrates, saps your skin of plumpness, and can lead to breakouts"*

# IF YOU A FLY GAL,
## get your nails done.
# GET A PEDICURE,
# GET YOUR HAIR DID.

*Missy Elliott*

# Bridal Trials
## THE ULTIMATE GUIDE

Getting the most out of your practice sessions

Your beauty team research should start seven or eight months before your wedding. Once you spot someone you like, check out their online portfolios, read reviews from previous brides and book a trial as early as six months before your wedding. Our top tip is to plan them around any events you have coming up, putting that professional hair and makeup to good use.

### Hair
Bring photos of the style you're after and your dress, so your stylist can see the neckline and vibe of your gown.

Ask your stylist's opinion about what suits your face shape - they are the experts. If you're not happy, speak up. It's a trial, which means it may not be perfect first time. Your feedback will allow your stylist to play around with it until you're both happy. If you never wear your hair up, there's no rule to say you have to start now. We're all for a bridal down-do.

Bring along hair accessories that you plan to wear, to see the finished look.

If you're changing colour, do this at least six months beforehand, to make sure you're happy with it.

### Makeup
Try to have your makeup trial on the same day as your hair trial, so you get a really good idea of the finished look. Just like your hair trial, it's helpful to bring pictures of your desired makeup look.

Tell your makeup artist what kind of finish you love, whether it's matte, dewy, full or light coverage.

If you don't normally wear much makeup, you might feel like your makeup is too much at first, but remember that it has to last all day and endure the stare of a camera and therefore needs to be kicked up a notch from a normal everyday look.

### Tan
You can't road-test your tan too much. It can be tricky to find the right treatment for your skin, so have a couple of trials in different salons.

If you're naturally fair, opt for a the palest shade on offer, to keep things natural and glowing.

Again, if you can arrange your tan trial to take place the day before your hair and makeup trials, you'll be able to see the full picture.

# YOUR WEDDING MAKEUP

## Finding the one

Lots of brides get makeup artist recommendations from friends and family. Book a few trials if you wish, and don't worry about offending anyone you're not happy with. Different artists have different styles, it's not one-size-fits-all.

## Communication is key

The key to developing a good rapport with your makeup artist is communication. How will they know you've got eyelids that don't hold shadow well unless you tell them? Equally, a makeup artist worth his or her salt will ask you lots of questions about your skin, how it reacts to things, what products you like and what products you hate. Here are some things you can do to make everything crystal clear:

1. Bring photos of what you'd like
2. Be realistic. If your picture is of Angelina Jolie but you have really thin lips, it's not likely she'll be able to recreate the look exactly. Likewise if you ask for a natural look but show your artist a picture of Kim Kardashian, well...
3. Tell them what you hated about any other makeup you've had done (brows too thick, too much blush, not enough liner etc.)
4. Don't be afraid to try something. Your makeup artist is a pro, so take their advice on board.

5. Be honest. If there's something they're doing that you don't like the look or feel of, let them know.

## Practically perfect

There are some practical things you can do to ensure your makeup is the best it can be.

1. Moisturise and prep your skin before trials.
2. Maintain good skincare for the year before your wedding.
3. Build a collection of good quality products that work for you so you can do your own makeup on the second day or other events around the wedding.

## Play it safe

Big changes (such as getting your brows tinted or Botox, for instance) should be done in good time so there are no surprises on the day of the wedding. Likewise, anything you're planning to have done for your wedding day, have it in place for your makeup trial too, to mimic conditions as closely as you can.

# YOUR WEDDING HAIR

Your wedding day is not the time to risk having a bad hair day. Getting your hair in pristine condition, with the help of someone who knows their stuff, is our advice, as well as the following...

### Get in early
Don't underestimate the advantage a bit of time can give you when it comes to achieving brilliant bridal hair. Find a stylist and colourist you're happy with as soon as you can, and book them in for hair prep in the lead up.

### It's a process
Whether you're changing colour, having extensions applied, or just want to make sure your cut is on-point, consistency is key. Make a plan of action for your cuts, colour, and extensions, building in time for trials (at least one, but preferably two).

### Be practical
You (and your hair stylist) can only work with what you've got. When choosing styles and accessories, think about how they'll work in YOUR hair and on YOUR wedding day.

### To extend or not
If you're considering extensions, chat to your stylist about what you need and how far in advance you should have them applied. We recommend application about one month before the big day to let them settle and to allow time for a hair trial with them in. Bonded or micro-beaded extensions start at around €300 and can go up to €750 or more, depending on how much hair you're having applied. You'll pay €100 to €200 for a quality clip-in piece.

### Treat yourself
All of the colouring, trials and extending can, and will, take a toll on your natural hair, so we recommend keeping up regular in-salon and home treatments in the lead-up to your wedding, to minimise damage. Olaplex (from about €30) is great for helping with breakage due to colour, and homecare masques from quality salon brands like Redken, Kérastase and Joico will help maintain shine, strength and durability.

### On the day...
You'll have had your trial, but if you look in the mirror on the day and there's anything you're not happy with, tell your stylist. You want to be as comfortable and 'you' as possible, and your stylist will understand that.

# YOUR WEDDING SMILE

Your hair is your crowning glory, your eyes are the windows to your soul, but your smile? That's where everyone's eyes will be fixed for the day of your wedding, and your aching jaw will attest to that. Here's how to get that smile gleaming...

## Whitening

With an in-practice treatment you can usually see noticeable results within an hour or so of having the treatment. However, if you're a big coffee or red wine drinker, home maintenance can help combat recurring discolouration. Bear in mind, your teeth need to be in full health (in terms of decay and gum disease) before any cosmetic dentistry can take place.

Is it safe? Yes. Under the supervision of trained dental professionals, teeth whitening is fine for both teeth and gums. The most common side effect is tooth and gum sensitivity, but your dentist will be able to advise you on whether you are a good candidate for whitening and they can also ensure that you are using the right concentration of whitening formula.

## Straightening

Invisalign is a treatment we hear a lot about on social media at the moment as bloggers and brides-to-be go about straightening their teeth. The system straightens teeth using a series of nearly invisible, removable aligners that are custom-made specifically for your teeth. As you replace each aligner every two weeks, your teeth will move. Little by little, week by week your teeth will gradually move towards the projected final position.

They're comfortable, clear and removable, which is great because there can be a reluctance to undergo teeth straightening with 'train tracks' as an adult. Treatment time varies a lot, depending on your teeth's condition, so it's good to get a consultation sooner rather than later (if it's something you're considering), to ensure you'll have the recommended time to complete your treatment.

## Veneers

If you really want to go all out and correct your smile with veneers and implants, it's a costly process, but the results can be amazing. A veneer is a custom-made, thin later of porcelain that is securely bonded to the front surface of your teeth. This is to recreate the natural shape and appearance of the tooth. A precisely coloured shade of porcelain is used to closely match the colour of your natural teeth.

# LASHES AND BROWS

### Lash extensions

Go big or go home on the lash front, we say. Lash extensions are a fantastic way to bring instant drama to your eye makeup and you're likely to pay anything from €80 to €150 depending on the quality of the product. They're amazing on honeymoon as you can wear minimal makeup and still look like you made an effort. When attending a lash appointment, go eye-makeup free and prepare for a nice, long, lie down, as application can take between one and two hours.

### LVL Enhance

If falsies aren't your thing, LVL is a lash treatment that works with your own lashes. Treatment takes 55 minutes and, unlike a normal lash perm, LVL straightens your lashes from the root, giving the appearance of much longer lashes. Your lashes are then tinted and results last six to eight weeks. It doesn't involve extensions, adhesive or mascara, so it's ideal for those looking for a more natural (but still impactful) finish. LVL Lashes are about €55 for an hour-long treatment, and you will need a patch test. Try Oslo Beauty (oslobeauty.ie) or a recommended salon near you.

### Perfect Shape brows

Never underestimate the power of the right brow shape – they frame your face and help make everything a little more symmetrical. We love The Brow Artist's (facebook.com/thebrowartistofficial) Perfect Shape treatment which uses a combo of carefully considered shaping and bespoke tinting with a variety of custom-blended tones. This isn't a permanent treatment, as the tint wears off, but it provides the perfect backdrop for your own pencilling efforts, and regular visits to your brow artist will result in fuller, more fabulous brows in the long run.

### Semi-permanent brows

Go a step further with semi-permanent brows which involve a form of micropigmentation. The pigment is placed just under the skin with a very fine needle and the results will last up to two years, adding thickness and definition to your natural shape and helping fill any gaps caused by over-plucking (damn you, the Nineties!) Again, the pigment will be custom-blended to suit your colouring. This treatment is also fantastic for anyone suffering with hair loss or alopecia.

# YOUR WEDDING GLOW

Even those who aren't seasoned tanners often want a healthy glow for their wedding day. Whether you're a pro or a first timer, use caution to avoid tan-tastrophes...

### Don't even think about it
Sunbeds are never, ever, worth it. Don't risk your health for the sake of aesthetics. Especially when faking it is so easy. Remember, too, that parched skin is not good skin and one outing on a sunbed can add years to your appearance and cancel out all the other good work you're doing. Just don't do it.

### Work on your skin
Before you put anything onto your skin, get it in great nick. Invest in a body brush and some gentle exfoliating products. Use both twice a week to clear away dead skin cells and encourage lymph drainage.

### Try, try again
Bear in mind it takes a good fortnight (if not longer) to completely rid your skin of a spray tan, so you'll need a good chunk of time for trials. Choose a few brands you want to try and get started early.

### Tan and makeup
Speak to your makeup artist – does he/she want you to have your face tanned? Do they want you to come tanned to your makeup trial?

### Bronzing basics
Go to the salon wearing loose clothing (no bras, jeans, tight socks or anything else that'll leave a mark on your skin) and flip-flops. Your tanner should offer you moisturiser for your hands, feet, knees and elbows – ask if they don't.

When leaving the salon, be aware of the weather, avoiding rain at all costs. If you're travelling by car, put a towel between your shoulder and seatbelt to avoid transfer.

### The final countdown
A minimum of two weeks out from your wedding, stop using developing tans - you'll want to be clear and smooth to take your wedding week tan perfectly.

For tanning novices, have your tan two evenings prior to your wedding. If your wedding is Saturday, get a spray on Thursday evening. Shower Friday morning, then apply a good layer of hydrating, oil-free moisturiser and wear loose-fitting clothes.

For confident tanners, the day before your wedding should be fine, showering and moisturising on the morning. Avoid using a loofa in the shower - simply wash with your hands and shower gel. The exception to this is the underarm area – it's worth giving a thorough scrub there to minimise any transfer onto your dress.

# Bridal Botox
## THE BIG QUESTIONS

### Do I need it?
Nope! You're gorgeous the way you are, but if you have lines that you'd love to see the back off and have the budget and inclination, a Botox treatment will take care of them.

### How soon should I have Botox before my wedding?
As with any procedure, it's good to have a trial run. As the effects last for three to six months, have a first round six months before your wedding. If you love it, you can have a top up with confidence nearer to the day. Have your last procedure three or four weeks beforehand.

### Will everyone know I've had it?
Hey, there's no shame in the game! But, if you don't want to admit you've had the procedure, nobody needs to know. Those frozen-faced folk you see have gone way overboard and, in the right hands, you won't look like that. You'll be you, only fresher.

### Does it hurt?
Yes, but it's entirely bearable and numbing cream will be applied first.

### Will I have bruising/swelling?
This varies from person to person. Some people experience slight bruising for a day or two, while others won't have any.

### Will I feel weird not being able to move my face?
The movements that are limited will feel totally normal – like not being able to move your ears, for example.

### How long does it last?
This depends on how animated your expressions are normally, but generally the procedure's results will last between three and six months.

### Do I need to keep getting it forever, once I start?
No. Botox gives your skin a break from the creases we create with certain movements. Should you decide to never get Botox again, your lines will simply reappear and you can always go again later if you decide to.

### How much does it cost?
This depends on the number of areas you're having treated and the amount of product being administered. A consultation will establish this.

### Where should I go to have it done?
You only have one face, so don't trust anyone but the most highly trained specialists with it. Consider reputable clinics such as the award-winning Renew Skin Clinic (renewclinic.ie), where you'll benefit from the years of experience of respected medical professionals.

# Men's Grooming

When it comes to wed-prep, lads don't get off scot-free either. Pay some attention to the following and you'll never dread looking back at those wedding photos...

## Bring in the professionals

Yes, you can do a perfectly good shave yourself. And yes, taking a home razor to your head might be fine for day-to-day. However, your wedding is a biggie, so treat it as such and go to see the experts.

Getting your usual haircut is fine, but get it at least a week before the wedding day – a little regrowth is almost always a good thing, so give it the time it needs.

Head to a great barber for a straight-edge, hot towel shave. It will set you back about €35 and makes a nice treat for you and your groomsmen on the morning of the wedding.

If you have a beard or rock some smart stubble, you don't have to shave just because you're getting married. But do go for an expert beard trim so any facial hair is tamed, pre-wedding. A trim, shape and some key product will keep your beard in check all day long.

## Manly manicure

A photo of your wedding ring slipping onto awful looking fingernails won't be something to cherish forever. Even if it's not usually your bag, a manicure will sort those cuticles right out and make sure you're proud to flash your new jewellery at the camera.

## Hair today

Nose hair, unibrows, knuckle fluff and any other unwanted hair needs either grooming or removal. Head to a waxing salon and ask for a tidy. If you need your ears done, let it happen. It hurts a little, but beauty is pain, my friend. Waxperts salons have a man-specific wax called First Mate that's made especially for those niggly bits (*waxperts.ie*).

## Sink your teeth in

If your teeth aren't looking their sparkliest, consider a whitening session in the run up. (*For more on that, slip to page 150.*)

## Face facts

We're not saying you have to go to a plinky-plonky spa and have flower petals thrown at your feet, but popping in for a targeted facial, even once, pre-wedding can do wonders. A good exfoliation, a mask and a bit of face massage is a thoroughly relaxing experience too. You might just enjoy it!

## Do your homework

When it comes to home skincare, you're more than likely using an all-in-one cleanser and moisturising occasionally. Stepping up this routine slightly will reap dividends. Adding a serum into the mix could perk your skin right up. If you need help deciding what to buy, chat to someone on the counters in pharmacies and they'll guide you. Consistency is key here – decide on a routine and stick to it. Start early and don't mess around with new products the week of your wedding. Oh, and up your water intake – it'll really help your skin.

## Makeup matters

Your wedding pictures will exist online and in real life forever, so if you've got the type of skin that goes bright red at the thought of being the centre of attention, consider a small amount of makeup. If there's a bride in the equation or you're hiring a makeup artist for your bridesmaids or Mam, they can add a bit of colour corrector to tone your redness down, a bit of under-eye concealer to hide the pints from the night before, and a bit of powder so that if you sweat, your shine will be kept at bay. Add a bit of eyebrow gel to control the stray hairs and you'll be like a new man!

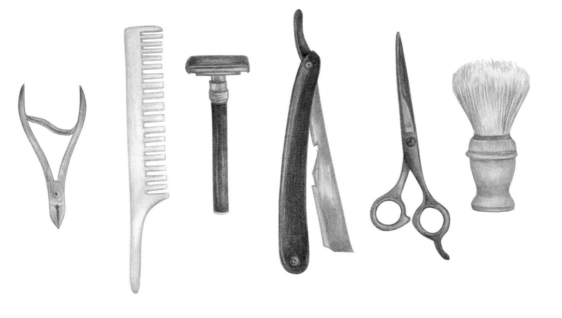

# Wedding Beauty Myths, Busted

From the moment you become engaged, nuggets of advice will come flying at you from every angle, about everything. When it comes to bridal beauty, some warnings are worth heeding, but some hold no water...

**You need to pack on the makeup**
Not true. Yes, you'll wear more than on a random Tuesday, but a longwearing look is about smart makeup, not lots and lots of it.

**Wearing red lipstick is a no-no**
If red lips are your go-to, your wedding day should be no different. Ask a bridesmaid to occasionally check your teeth for you, stick to the air kisses and you're golden.

**A facial the week of your wedding will lead to a breakout**
Not necessarily. You'll know yourself if you have skin that's prone to breaking out. If your skin is susceptible to very subtle changes, avoid it. But if getting facials is something you regularly do without issue, it should be fine. Avoid using things like Retinol or harsh peels for the very first time on the week of your wedding.

**You need a touch-up kit with you**
You really don't. Pack a lipstick for topping up and some pressed powder, but other than that, if your makeup artist did a good enough job and set your makeup well, it won't budge too much. And the last thing you want is a bronzer disaster all over your lovely white dress.

**You have to have...**
This pretty much applies to anything anybody says you have to do at your wedding – ignore the noise. If you hate the feel of fake lashes, go without - there are other ways to define your eyes. If your makeup artist is insisting on matte lipstick, but you prefer gloss, hold your ground. They can wear matte lipstick at their own wedding if they like!

# Confetti loves...
## SELECTED SUPPLIERS

**NIAMH MARTIN MAKEUP - CREATIVE BRIDAL ARTIST**
NIAMHMARTIN.COM
NIAMHMARTINMAKEUP@GMAIL.COM

**DAVID MCCONVILLE - SPECIALIST ORTHODONTICS**
TEL: 071 915 0820
DAVIDMCCONVILLEORTHODONTICS.IE

**SARAH GAYNOR NAILS**
TEL: 086 212 0942
SARAHGAYNORNAILS@GMAIL.COM

**BROWS BY NOELLA**
INSTAGRAM: @browsbynoella
BROWSBYNOELLA@GMAIL.COM

# Beauty notes

# Décor & Details

## BRINGING THAT PINTEREST
## BOARD TO LIFE

# The Devil's In The Details

Ah the fun, creative part. The gorgeous, personal details and dreamy décor that make up the visuals of your wedding. Think crafting sessions with your bridesmaids over something sparkling, making moodboards and conjuring up ideas for unique touches your guests will love - yay! But pay heed, DIY can take a dark turn when you take on too much. Particularly if you're not generally a crafty person and especially if you leave it until the last minute. A new sparkler on your hand does not Martha Stewart make, so if it's generally not your bag, leave it to someone else from the get-go to avoid falling down the rabbit hole.

There's a very simple way of establishing if something's worth doing. Make one paper flower and time yourself doing so. If it takes you two minutes, and you need 800 of them to make that epic installation you've envisioned for your altar... that's 26 hours, friend. Even with a team of the craftiest bridesmaids around you, that will get old super quick and, at certain points, the title of this piece might feel all too real, and you'll start to question whether Satan actually does have a hand in proceedings.

But if you're up to the challenge and relish the thought of gathering gorgeous goodies that will all go into creating your unique vision, you'll be in your element here. In this chapter, we aim to help you establish your own personal wedding style and discuss the finer details of décor. We talk cakes, florals, stationery and all the other creative parts that make up your day. Our advice? Have fun with it and don't be afraid to dream big!

*Good luck!*

# Finding Your Wedding Style

The frantic pinning of all the things has, no doubt, commenced. But, when you love the look of everything you see on Pinterest, how do you decide what's really for you and avoid having a hodgepodge of ten different styles in one day? Read on, party people...

### Establish the bigger picture

Certain things will help direct the look and feel of a wedding, your venue being the main one. Planning a black tie ball in a rustic barn, for example, might be a stretch (although we actually think that sounds like gas craic). Playing up the style of your venue and working with the existing colour scheme will make for a more cohesive look.

### Get inspired

Wedding magazines and websites (*Confetti* and *confetti.ie*, obvs) and sites such as Pinterest are obvious sources of wedding inspiration, but don't be afraid to think outside the box. If fashion is your passion or you're an art buff, draw inspiration from your favourite style of painting or the aesthetic of a designer you love, as a basis for your theme. It'll help you establish a unique colour palette and vibe that's truly you.

### Stay in lane

If you've established a very particular theme and feel, try not to get too distracted. You'll encounter so many ideas and new wedding trends will emerge with every season that passes in the lead up, but stick to your guns and don't be tempted to confuse things with late, random additions.

### Throw out the rule book

Alternatively, if your tastes are eclectic and you love the idea of a colourful celebration with mix-and-match elements of everything you love, go for it! Rules are made to be broken.

*"Playing up the style of your venue and working with the existing colour scheme will make for a more cohesive look"*

# DO I NEED A WEDDING STYLIST?

While a wedding planner's role is centred on logistics, a stylist is all about the aesthetic. They look after the design of the wedding, including everything from floor plans to the flowers and linens. Those may sound like small details, but a stylist's main job is to give your event a cohesive look that suits whatever theme or style you have in mind. These questions will help you decide if you need one...

### How busy are you?

If you're happy to give up your weekends to sourcing props and figuring out the best details to create the perfect ambiance, you might have a lot of fun with this. However, if you're already run off your feet or have a short planning timeframe, this may be a job for a professional who already has a sourcebook, plenty of props at their disposal and experience with all sorts of different styles.

### How much time will you have in your reception room before the event?

If there's an event at your venue the day before, your reception room might need to be dressed on the morning of your wedding, which could prove quite stressful and rob you of your lovely, relaxed wedding morning with your crew.

### How much do you care about the 'look' of your wedding?

The more you think you'll agonise over the aesthetic details of your wedding, the more you'll get out of a stylist. If you're great on logistics but not on the creative front, a stylist may be more helpful than a planner.

### How detail-orientated are you?

There are a lot of small elements that bring together a big event and if you're not known for being super organised with great attention to detail, this may be tricky for you. Have you already thought about ceremony décor and where you'll put your guest book? Then you're all good. If those kinds of decisions fill you with dread, a stylist is your only man.

### Are you easily overwhelmed?

With Pinterest at your fingertips, it's easy to become overwhelmed with the sheer amount of inspiration out there. If you've a clear vision of what exactly you want and how you'll achieve it – perfect. Some finesse and clever decision-making is all you need.

### Are you getting married abroad?

Planning a wedding at home is hard enough but figuring out how to source props and décor internationally is another level. Having someone on the ground who knows your venue and who can coordinate all your décor bits from your destination will be a godsend.

# D.I.Why?
## WHAT TO TRY AND WHAT TO BUY

Not matter how crafty you are, wedding projects can very quickly turn from D.I.Y to D.I.why did I start this? Personal projects are a lovely way to give your day a unique touch, but there are some things – for your own sanity – that should be left to the experts.

## WHAT TO TRY

### Placecards
As DIY projects go, placecards are reasonably doable. Get your best handwriting pen out and if your placecards double as escort cards, you've killed two birds and taken both items off your stationery bill.

### Table décor
DIY decorating your entire venue might be more hassle than it's worth, but you can take standard table centrepieces to the next level with floral touches, votives and candles in various shapes and sizes.

### Signage
Signs directing guests from the ceremony to your reception are a fun project to create yourself and it means you can personalise them – a sweet touch.

## WHAT TO BUY

### Favours
Favours can be DIY'd but you have to draw a line on what's reasonable. Planning on packaging up little pots of homemade jam for each guest?

They can be prepared in advance and will hold for months, so they're perfect. Want to give each guest a little box of home-baked cookies? You'll likely have to spend all day in the kitchen the day before your wedding, which won't be ideal.

### Floral arrangements
Great flowers aren't cheap, so you'd be forgiven for trying to save a few quid by heading to the flower market and doing them yourself. But, in our experience, this is a huge, time consuming job and the small savings (you still have to buy the flowers) may not be worth it. Also, Ireland is filled with some incredibly talented floral artists whose work you'll adore, so it's worth hiring an expert. Shave a few quid off the bill by choosing in-season blooms, instead.

### Big scale décor
You might love the idea of a million origami pieces creating a backdrop for your reception, but after making about 20, you'll probably have had enough. Instead, purchase the parts and enlist the help of staff at your venue, your bridal party and family and friends to set it all up.

# Flowers By Season

Before you set your heart on that peony bouquet you saw on Instagram, make sure your chosen blooms are available at the time of your wedding. Here's a quick breakdown of when each flower is at their best...

## Spring
When spring has sprung in Ireland, colourful florals and leafy green foliage come to life.

Cherry Blossom
Clematis
Hyacinth
Parrot Tulip
Ranunculus
Protea
Garden Rose
Scented Eucalyptus

## Autumn
Warmer colours start to creep in now and look wonderful teamed with some rustic foliage or berries.

Gerbera Daisy
Garden Rose
Sunflower
Anemone
Dahlia
Delphinium
Amaranthus
Rose Hip

## Summer
High summer will, of course, bring an abundance of options. Make the most of beautiful blooms that won't hang around.

Baby's Breath
Gardenia
Hydrangea
Lily
Chrysanthemum
Peony
Scabiosa
Sweet Pea

## Winter
Some more imagination is needed now, but we adore a beautiful winter bouquet! Chat to your florist about different options in colder months.

Succulents
Bellis
Icelandic Poppy
Calla Lily
Thistle
Amaryllis
Tulip
Orchid

# In YOUR ARMS I'D STAY
*forever if I could,*
## FOREVER IF I MAY

*Ryan Adams*

# Wedding Cakes 101

This is one of the more fun parts of wedding planning – what's not to love about tasting cake? Whether you're a traditional, fondant three-tier cake couple or you're drawn to stacked wheels of delicious Irish cheese, there's a wedding cake out there for you (and you'll have a great time finding it!)

## Cutting edge

Traditionally, the cake cutting takes place towards the end of the meal, just before the dancing begins, to signify that the formalities of the reception are over. Of course, you don't have to conform to this, or any other rule.

## You've been served

Generally, cake is either served in lieu of dessert, with tea and coffee or saved for later on and served with your night bites. It's also popular to save it for day two, providing a welcome sugar rush for second day revellers. It's an old tradition for couples to save the top fruit tier of the cake to share on their first anniversary. If you're going down that road, make sure you let your venue know not to cut it up.

## Lasting moment

How long will your cake last? This depends on the filling and icing. If you opt for a fondant fruit cake, it should last much longer due to the alcohol content in the fruit mixture. If it's a cream-filled sponge cake, it's best to make sure it's eaten by day two. Sounds like a challenge!

## Cake that

Here's a little breakdown of the different styles.

◇ **Fondant**
Traditionally a fruit cake, covered in a smooth, stiff icing.

◇ **Buttercream**
A soft, workable icing with a textured finish.

◇ **Naked**
A naked cake is a tiered sponge cake, usually with a cream filling.

◇ **Semi-Naked**
A lot like a naked cake, but finished with a transparent, iced coating.

◇ **Donuts or macarons**
For non-traditional couples, a donut or a macaron tower is an excellent option. Have it disassembled once the photos are done, and guests can serve themselves.

◇ **Cheese Cake**
This is for couples who are more savoury than sweet-toothed. You can build up tiers of your favourite cheeses, decorate with fruit or flowers and serve later as a cheese board for guests. Try Sheridans Cheesemongers (*sheridanscheesemongers.com*) or SuperValu (*supervalu.ie*).

# Wedding Stationery
## YOUR COMPLETE GUIDE

We're kinda obsessed with stationery and pretty paperie around these parts. Your wedding suite is made up of lots of pieces, including essentials like Save The Dates, invites, RSVP cards and optional extras.

### Save The Dates
Your Save The Dates are a little heads up to your guests that you're getting hitched. They can be sent out anywhere from three to twelve months before the wedding and should include the date and some brief information on the location. They're particularly helpful for any guests who are travelling from out-of-town, or if you're having a destination do.

### Wedding invitations
The most important component, the formal notice, inviting your guests to your wedding ceremony and reception. It should include details of the date, ceremony and reception location (if different) and times. *For more detailed information, check out our guide on page 132.*

### Evening invitations
These are for guests who are not attending the main reception, but joining you later for dancing and drinks. They usually look much like your full invitations, and should give information on the time and reception location.

### RSVP cards
These are sent with your invitations, allowing guests to let you know whether or not they are attending.

### Directions card
It's always helpful to give your out-of-town guests more information on the location of your venue. If you think your venue will be slightly difficult to find, include exact coordinates so people can key them into sat navs or Google Maps.

## Order of Service/ceremony booklet

Your ceremony booklet gives your guests the full running order of the ceremony. It should contain the name of the officiant, names of the bridal party, songs or music, poems and readings. They will differ slightly between religious, civil, spiritualist and humanist ceremonies, but the general layout will be quite similar.

## Table plan

Your table plan should be on display either in the main lobby or foyer of your venue, or just outside the reception room. It will inform your guests what table they are being seated at and who they'll be sitting with.

## Table names/numbers

These will be placed on each table. Numbers or names are used to identify each table, corresponding with your table plan.

## Place cards

These are name cards at each place setting with your guests' names on them, informing each person which seat is theirs.

## Menu cards

Menu cards inform your guests of the delicious meal they're about to be served. There can be two choices for the main course, and staff will circulate before the meal to note each guest's preference.

## Thank you cards

Your thank you cards are usually sent out shortly after the wedding and before you embark on your honeymoon, to thank your guests for their gift and for celebrating the day with you.

"Save The Dates... They're particularly helpful for any guests who are travelling from out-of-town, or if you're having a destination do"

# Décor Extras

Deadly design details are a brilliant way of making a venue
your own and really injecting your personalities into proceedings.
Here are a few extras to consider...

## Lighting
This tends to be overlooked and, in our opinion, lighting is one of the most important décor elements at your wedding. If your reception room is badly lit, it will reflect in the mood and in your photos. Hiring in some key lighting to brighten up the space can create a magical ambiance.

## Giant initials
Who doesn't want to see their name in lights? A fun décor extra, have them placed just outside your reception room to greet guests, or beside the dance floor for a nightclub feel. An awesome variation on this theme is a fresh, floral version. From oversized, pastel creations to vibrant, tabletop varieties, they're a gorgeous addition to your wedding décor.

## Flower wall
These are, no doubt, a stand-out piece and they make for fantastic photo booth backdrops or ceremony focal points. There are various forms of flower walls, from dainty hanging single stem blooms, to full-on walls of Kim K proportions. Incorporate your wedding palette into the colours of the blooms – for example, if you're having a black tie affair, opt for a full white flower wall with black accents – slick!

## Floral installations
There are so many incredible things you can do with flowers to add to your reception décor. Opt for a floral arch for either the ceremony space, or over the entrance to your reception room, or go for a more subtle approach with pressed flower table numbers. They're super easy to create yourself with some empty frames, by simply inserting the blooms of your choice. You can then write the table numbers on the glass with paint or markers. Cute!

## Balloons
We're obsessed with balloons and, let's face it, who isn't? You can easily jazz up an otherwise plain venue with this fun wedding trend. If you're not that into lavish centrepieces, fun confetti-filled balloons are perfect for popping on your tables instead. You could also arrange for an over-the-top balloon arch or installation to add an extra element of fun to your wedding reception.

## Fun signage

This will work especially well if you're having an outdoor or festival themed wedding. Things to include are bar signs, ceremony and reception signs, toilet signs and photobooth or entertainment area signs.

## Dessert/cocktail table backdrop

You can easily jazz up a boring dessert table, candy cart or cocktail-making station with some fun, colourful tassels carefully placed around the front of the tables. Or, opt for a funky fringe curtain or twinkling fairy lights to hang up behind the table.

## Donut wall

Donuts are dominating weddings right now and we can't think of a more fun (and delicious) décor element than a donut wall. Tasty, doughy rings with pretty pastel designs and sugar flowers adorning a brightly coloured wall, will arguably be the most Instagrammable part of your whole wedding and doubles up as dessert – winning!

# Making It Personal

Incorporating personal touches that involve you and your guests is
a really gorgeous way of making everyone feel included and special.
Here are some of our favourite ideas...

### Escort cards
Finding your table number can be
a fun moment for guests so why not
take this a step further? Surprise your
guests with their own smiling faces by
using a photo of you with each guest
as their place setting, or put their name
on a rolled up scroll with a memory
or anecdote written inside about a
time you spent together. It's a sweet
memento they can take home, and
a lovely way to help your guests feel
connected to your day.

### Photo wall
We're not talking a 21st birthday style
wall of embarrassment here. Instead,
share your favourite moments from
your relationship, including photos with
attending family and friends, to show
them how much a part of your story
they are. Set up mismatched framed
photos or create a 'washing line' of
photos with pics of your guests from
over the years, making your photo
display double as décor.

### Love story
Everyone in the room knows one or
both of you, but they might not know
the details of your love story, like when
and where you met, or even the story of
your engagement. Creating a love story
board is a great way of paying homage
to your journey to being married and
a fun way to give guests a little history
lesson on how it all came to be.

### Chair décor
Mr & Mrs (or Mr & Mr / Mrs & Mrs) signs
on your chairs are sweet details, but
you can go one better by personalising
them. If you've got cute pet names for
one another, write them on chalk signs
and hang them on your respective
chairs, or pop cute childhood pics of
each of you on the back.

### Favourite things
Our friends and family all know us for
our obsessions, so why not incorporate
some into your big day? Cheese
obsessed? Opt for a cheese wheel
rather than traditional cake. Known for
a quirky drink of choice? Have it as your
signature cocktail. Got a severe case
of wanderlust or forever quoting your
favourite TV show? Make your table
names references to places you've been
or TV shows you love.

# Confetti loves...
## SELECTED SUPPLIERS

**CUPCAKES AND COUNTING**
TEL: 085 779 0310
CUPCAKESANDCOUNTING.COM

Do things differently.

Go paperless for invites.

**BE OUR GUEST**
WEDDING GUEST APP
BEOURGUEST.APP

**KELLY LOU CAKES**
TEL: 087 953 0681
KELLYLOU.COM

# Décor notes

# Destination Weddings

## WE'RE OUTTA HERE!

# What goes on tour

I f the lure of guaranteed good weather, spectacular light and a holiday vibe is too much to resist, you may well be considering a destination do. There's something unmistakably special about heading off to the sun with your crew, to celebrate your love story. Your wedding becomes much more than a one-day affair, with festivities often beginning from the second you land on foreign soil. And the days afterwards are some of the most relaxing and love-filled you're likely to experience.

First up, we'll take a look at some of the top spots chosen by Irish couples each year and a few new ideas to inspire. We'll also discuss the perks and pitfalls of getting hitched abroad and offer up some top tips we've picked up along the way.

If you're thinking about heading away to say 'I do', there are of course some extra considerations to plan for. In this chapter we'll cover off the all-important legalities around getting married in each place and the requisite timings involved. There's no denying that getting married abroad can be a complicated process, but we've broken it down country-by-country, so you're forearmed.

...Everyone you love partying hard in the one place, in holiday mode, and it's all for you? Sounds pretty dreamy to us.

Bon voyage!

# Getting Married Abroad
## POPULAR DESTINATIONS FOR IRISH COUPLES

Every year, many Irish couples gather their troops and fly to the sun to marry. Here are the seven most popular dreamy destinations and what you can expect from each...

### France

If you're looking for an urban and romantic wedding, consider Paris, The City of Love. It really is, as the name suggests, one of the most romantic places in the world. It has a sense of familiarity to it meaning that, from the second you arrive, it almost feels like home. Or, opt for a stunning château in the picturesque French countryside of Provence. It immediately conjures up images of lush, green, vineyards and sweet-smelling lavender fields, as far as the eye can see. The best time to marry in France is between May and September, for an almost-guaranteed glorious day.

### Italy

The food, the wonderful people and the weather are three reasons Italy is one of the most attractive wedding destinations for Irish couples. With its mountainous backdrops, the Adriatic coast and that covet-able climate, it's one of the most picturesque places in the world. You could visit the small city of Florence a hundred times and still discover something new each time. The wine-rich hills overlooking the breathtaking old city make for the perfect destination. Travel further south for all the beauty that the Amalfi Coast has to offer. Sorrento and Positano both boast azure-blue water, colourful buildings dotted on hillsides and untouched sleepy villages. The best time to visit is April to September for warm weather and long, light-filled days.

### Spain

For most, Spain conjures up images of sun, sea, sand and memories of glorious holidays. As a destination wedding option, it boasts stunning hidden gems in the Spanish hillsides, beautiful architecture, picturesque vineyards and a Mediterranean climate. The months of April to June are great as they're warm, but not too hot. Why not base yourself in the seaside locations of Benalmádena or Marbella, and venture to one of the many hidden gems in the Spanish countryside for your big day? Dreaming of an island wedding? Well, while you may associate Ibiza with the hedonistic holidays of your youth, it's also a stunningly beautiful island with peaceful towns and unspoiled coast.

## Portugal

Boasting some of the best beaches in Europe, sprawling vineyards, elegant venues, great cuisine and even better wine, Portugal is both a picturesque and practical choice. Their wedding season kicks off in spring and winds down around October. You may be familiar with destinations along the Algarve, such as Albufeira and Lagos, both of which are dotted with beautiful venues for your wedding. If you're looking for something with a little more character, Portugal's hilly, coastal capital of Lisbon is one of the oldest cities in the world. It is instantly recognisable by the old city's pastel-coloured buildings, encompassing modern culture, but maintaining its unique heritage and traditions.

## Malta

Malta's popularity as a destination-wedding location has grown rapidly in recent years. There are many reasons, including Malta's temperate climate, the ease of travel and its historic old towns. The island's original capital, Mdina is a tiny walled town, also know as The Silent City. You could walk around the town in just under a half an hour, but be sure to savour and soak up the beauty that it has to offer. Or, if you're looking for an island option, the second-largest in the archipelago of Malta is the scenic Gozo, boasting orange-red sands. The best time to wed in Malta is between late May and June, when you'll get glorious, uninterrupted sunshine.

## Croatia

With beautiful views, wonderful locations and historic settings, it's easy to see why Croatia is a popular choice. The months where you will get the most out of the weather are May to September. Get married in the beautiful historic town of Dubrovnik with its marble streets, baroque buildings and turquoise seas. The Old Town is one of the world's most famous towns, surrounded by stone walls dating back to the 16th century. Another wonderful option is the island of Hvar, which features beautiful beaches such as Dubovica and stunning, vast lavender fields.

## Slovenia

With more than half of its surface covered in forest, Slovenia has to win the award for the most Disney destination. It's a magical combination of green vistas and clear lakes, with cascading mountains providing a beautiful backdrop. In northwest Slovenia lies Lake Bled, in the Julian Alps. Surrounded by mountains and forests, medieval Bled Castle towers intimidatingly over the lake, on the north shore. With regards to climate, you can expect very cold winters and moderately warm summers. Alternatively, situated on the coast, is the warm and sunny coastal resort of Portorož. It combines the best of Slovenia's dreamy, fairytale backdrop with the seaside appeal of a Mediterranean country.

*YOUR LOVE IS KING,*

*crown you in
my heart*

Sade

# DESTINATION WEDDINGS
## Perks & Pitfalls

## YAY!

### (Don't) take the weather with you
The first and most obvious benefit of marrying practically anywhere except Ireland is that the weather is likely to be better. Dining al fresco, dancing in the moonlight and drinks receptions on sprawling lawns – the dream!

### Let there be light
A bright, dry day with plentiful daylight hours means gorgeous, colourful wedding photographs that flatter everything from you to your venue and everything else in between.

### Less is more
Depending how you do it, your destination wedding is likely to be less expensive than marrying in Ireland, with many venue, food and drinks costs coming in far below Irish prices.

### Different strokes
In a year when lots of pals are getting married, your destination wedding will certainly stand out from the rest. It'll offer up a very different experience for not only you, but for your family and your guests as well.

## BOO!

### Absent friends
Whether it's new babies, finances, illness or old age, there are bound to be some pals who can't make it. Before you let that rule it out entirely, keep in mind that the same will apply to an Irish wedding – you will never please everyone or pick a date that 100% of your desired guests can make. You can always have another smaller party when you get home; an excuse to do it all over again – yay!

### Planning blind
If you can swing it, we always recommend a couple of recce trips. But there will always be elements of a destination do that you're booking blind. Trust your wedding planner, vendor's reviews and your gut and just go for it.

### A wash out
Your sun-drenched dreams might be dashed if you're unlucky enough to experience inclement weather at your beach resort venue or outdoor vineyard setting. A plan B is vital, as is a good attitude. It'll still be a blast, so just go with the flow.

# Destination Weddings
## THE LEGAL BIT

The legalities of marrying abroad will differ from country to country, so it's important to do your research. Here's our quick guide – you can find out more on *citizensinformation.ie* and by contacting the civil registration office of the country you're planning to marry in...

### France

Getting legally married in France isn't as easy as in other countries, unfortunately. In France, there is a 40-day residency requirement if you wish to have a civil ceremony. You and/or your partner must be living in France for a minimum of 30 days, plus an additional 10 days for paperwork, before the wedding. However, there may be ways of getting around this, for example if you, or a member of your family, have property in France the local Mayor may make an exception at their own discretion but that's not a guarantee. Religious ceremonies are not legally binding under French law, but you can have a civil ceremony at home in Ireland and a beautiful blessing in France.

### Italy

In Italy, you are permitted to have civil, Catholic and same-sex ceremonies. While there's no official residency requirement for civil ceremonies, Catholic ceremonies are not permitted in either Capri or Sorrento if neither one of you are permanent residents. You will need to obtain a 'Nulla Osta', prior to the wedding. This translates as your Freedon to Marry certificate, granting you permission to marry in Italy. All original documents, such as passports and legal papers, will need to be accompanied by Italian translations. Don't apply for documents and certs more than six months before the wedding, as they'll have expired under Italian regulations. Any documents will need to be presented to the town hall a number of days before the wedding, so plan to arrive at least two days in advance. If you're using a wedding planner, they'll be able to do all of this for you.

### Spain

If you're Catholic, having a religious ceremony in Spain is relatively straightforward. In fact, a Catholic wedding is the only way to be legally married in Spain if you don't reside there. For other religions or civil ceremonies, you may have a blessing, but the paperwork will have to be done at home, unless one of you is a Spanish citizen, as there is a two-year residency requirement. Sounds like a good excuse for another party at home, we reckon!

## Portugal
In Portugal, civil and Catholic ceremonies are the only legally recognised ceremonies and both types of ceremonies should be conducted in Portuguese, so it's a good idea to hire an interpreter. If you're opting for a Catholic ceremony, be mindful that once you've received approval from your chosen priest, the wedding must take place within three months.

## Malta
The great news is that getting married in Malta is pretty straightforward. You'll need to register your intent to marry online, supplying specific information and then appear in person before the ceremony at the Marriage Registry in Valletta, to confirm details and finalise matters. If your ceremony is taking place in Gozo, you're advised to also contact Gozo Public Registry. Log on to *visitmalta.com* for any further information you may need.

## Croatia
Getting married in Croatia is pretty simple, but there are a few binding rules and regulations that you'll need to bear in mind. If you're having a religious ceremony, you'll need to provide proof you have been legally married in a civil ceremony, either in Croatia or at home. You don't need to be resident in Croatia to get married there, but you do need to make an appointment to meet the Maticar (registrar) a few days before your wedding – so factor that into your itinerary. You'll need all of your documentation, birth certificates and passports to hand. All documentation will need to be translated into Croatian – and most ceremonies are in Croatian too, so you'll need a translator.

## Slovenia
There are certain steps you'll need to take when getting married in Slovenia – and bear in mind that, should you go down the religious route, you'll need to have a civil ceremony first. Only a civil ceremony is considered valid in Slovenia. You'll need to register the marriage in the town in which you wish to get married, at the Marriage Registry Office. You can do this from six months to two weeks ahead of your wedding (but, like all things, the sooner the better). They'll need some documentation, too: original birth certificates, passports, a Certificate of Freedom to Marry – and all documents not in Slovene need to be accompanied by a translation, done by a certified translator.

# TOP TIPS

## Get a planner!

We can't overstate this; a wedding planner is almost always vital when planning a destination wedding. Their local knowledge is invaluable, as is their relationship with vendors and ability to get you the best deal. They're not just your woman/man on the ground before the date, they'll also take care of everything on the day, so you can relax.

## Consider a holiday website

Distance brings extra logistics and having plenty of helpful information about locations, accommodation and travel options available to your guests is a great idea. It will really help them out and save you answering the same question lots of times. They're also fun to populate and will help build the excitement. See more on this on page 136.

# Confetti loves...
## SELECTED SUPPLIERS

**PLANNED BY TARA - DESTINATION WEDDINGS MALTA**
PLANNEDBYTARA.IE
TARA@PLANNEDBYTARA.IE

ITALY
**CASTELBRANDO**
TEL: +39 0438 9761
CASTELBRANDO.IT

GREECE
**ST. NICOLAS BAY RESORT HOTEL & THALASSA VILLAS LUXURY VILLAS AT THE WATERFRONT**
TEL: +30 28410 90200
STNICOLASBAY.GR - THALASSAVILLAS.GR

# Destination Wedding notes

# Honeymoons

## IT'S THE HUMIDITY!

# If We Took A Holiday...

Honeymoons are a lifesaver in so many ways. In the run-up to your wedding, they're a great way of seeing beyond the day, when it's all you can think about. When your world revolves around getting hitched, it acts as a helpful and important reminder that there's life afterwards. They're also the only known cure for the post-wedding crash, giving you something else to look forward to, even if you're not heading off right away.

All holidays are wonderful, of course, but the togetherness of your first big trip as newlyweds is pretty remarkable. You'll feel like a mini travelling team. It's often a much-needed break from the madness too. After all, organising a wedding whilst working, bringing up kids, or whatever else keeps you busy, is no mean feat. No doubt you'll have earned the break as you set off on your adventure to far-flung climes, together.

Planning your honeymoon is another big job on the list but we hope this chapter will help guide you through it with ease, making the only tricky part deciding which paradise to travel to.

The choice can be a little overwhelming, so we've put together a hit-list of the top destinations for Irish couples and what you can expect from each. Together with our guides on what to do before you go, what to pack and some important things to note, you'll be all set. Take us with you?

*Happy travels!*

# Things To Do Before You Go

The madness of the wedding is over and you're looking forward to chilling out big-time on your honeymoon. Hold your horses though; you have a job or two to box off before you go! Sorting out this little lot will mean you can jet off with a clear mind and a fully ticked 'to do' list.

### Send off your forms
Unless you're looking for a good excuse to do it all over again, you need to send your marriage registration forms to the HSE within 30 days of your ceremony.

### Have your wedding dress cleaned
The sooner you get your dress to a specialist cleaner, the less time any little stains have to settle in. If you're leaving shortly after your wedding, ask your maid of honour to do this.

### Return the suits
The return of rental suits is often the best man's job, so make sure to get your groom's suit to him if applicable.

### Open your gifts
This one should be easy to remember. But don't forget to make a list of what everyone gave you, so you can write personalised thank you cards when the time comes.

### Send thank you cards
If you can bare it, get this labour-intensive job out of the way before you jet off. Don't forget to send cards to your lovely suppliers as well as your guests.

### Pay suppliers
If there are outstanding payments to be made, be cool and do this before you swan off to the sun.

### Collect décor
If you brought props and decorative items to dress your venue, collect them after the wedding, or ask a friend to do so.

### Distribute your wedding cake
If you have large slabs of cake left, make sure to box it up and share it amongst family before it goes bad.

### Say your thanks
As well as thank you cards to your guests, make sure to take the time to call or pay a visit to your bridesmaids and anyone else who had a big hand in organising the day. Anyone who has been a bridesmaid knows that it can feel like a part-time job, so a sincere thanks will be appreciated.

### Pack the essentials
Packing for your honeymoon before the wedding is a great idea. *Tick off our checklist on page 224* and then simply sail off into the sunset with your new husband or wife – woohoo!

# TRAVEL AGENT VS. BOOKING ONLINE

While honeymoon planning sounds much more fun and chilled than actual wedding planning, fair warning, it can be just as stressful. If you plan to go away straight after your wedding, try to get the honeymoon nailed down around six to eight months before the big day. But should you book it online yourself, or to take a little pressure off and hand the reins to a travel agent?

## Do it yourself honeymoon

After researching destinations, chat about what the dream honeymoon would be and settle on a destination. Once that's decided, you can start your in-depth research of the place. Things to look into are whether or not you need vaccinations, flight prices, travel insurance, airport transfers and accommodation. It comes as no surprise that you can find plenty of great deals online, if you dig around long enough. If you're a particularly organised and internet savvy person, you may find the researching and bargain hunting no problem and you might end up saving yourself a few quid. However, if the thought of another budget-managing task makes you want to run for the hills, you might be best with a travel agent, who can handle all of this in one fell swoop.

## With a little help from my friends

Firstly, find a travel agent that you're comfortable with - good agents should be patient, entertain your preferences with an open mind, and present a range of options. Research before you visit so you have an idea of where you want to go and the time of year. One of the benefits of a travel agent is that they have insider, first-hand knowledge on destinations and the deals or discounts available. If you're planning a multi-city honeymoon, save yourself the stress of booking several different flights and hotels, by having a travel agent do it for you. With so many tickets and reservations to keep track of, it can all get a bit messy and overwhelming, so it's nice to know that someone else can just handle it without accidentally booking something for the wrong day or airport. Plus, if mishaps happen while you're away, you have someone you can contact right away.

# What To Pack

**Carry-on bag**
◇ Boarding passes
◇ Passports
◇ Hotel confirmations
◇ Driver's licence
◇ Debit/credit cards
◇ Local currency (if necessary)
◇ Vaccination documents
◇ Any medication needed
◇ Contraception
◇ Painkillers
◇ Sunglasses
◇ Camera
◇ Chargers and travel adapters
◇ Small toiletry bag with essentials
◇ Any valuable jewellery items
◇ Books/magazines
◇ Headphones
◇ Change of clothes

**Check-in bag**
◇ Toiletry bag
◇ Makeup bag
◇ Suncream and after-sun
◇ Insect repellent
◇ Mini travel first aid kit
◇ Hair curlers/straighteners
◇ Day bag/backpack
◇ 2-3 pairs of shoes/sandals
◇ Shorts
◇ Trousers
◇ Skirts/dresses
◇ Casual tops
◇ Evening tops

◇ Underwear
◇ Socks
◇ Swimwear
◇ Evening wrap/jacket
◇ Evening bag
◇ Accessories
◇ Sleepwear
◇ Runners and gym gear (if so inclined!)

**Add ons for beach honeymoon**
◇ Sun dresses
◇ Beach bag
◇ Sun hat
◇ Flip-flops

**Add ons for winter/skiing honeymoon**
◇ Waterproof ski pants and jacket
◇ Heavy jumpers
◇ Under layers
◇ Ski gloves
◇ Warm hat/headband
◇ Neck warmer/scarf
◇ Ski goggles
◇ Ski socks
◇ Waterproof boots

**Add ons for sightseeing/safari honeymoon**
◇ Comfortable walking shoes
◇ Mosquito netting
◇ Binoculars
◇ Neutral-coloured clothing
◇ Safari/sun hat

# My Packing List

# I need a fiancé
## CUTE AS BEYONCÉ

*Nelly*

# VACCINATION STATIONS

If you're planning on venturing to one of the more tropical parts of the world for your honeymoon, you may need to get vaccinated. There are many types and requirements, so we've put together this quick guide. For everything you need to know about being vaccinated in Ireland, log on to the Tropical Medical Bureau's website, *tmb.ie*

### Why should I get vaccinated?
Travelling to exotic parts of the world is a rewarding and often once-in-a-lifetime experience, but make sure you're protected while there. Certain areas have illnesses and diseases not commonly seen on Irish shores, such as malaria or polio. There are some vaccines that are recommended and not strictly mandatory but, the last thing you want is to fall ill on honeymoon, so it's best to err on the side of caution.

### What do I need?
When you're considering your honeymoon destination, be sure to read up on the different vaccinations, as specific recommendations will, of course, vary from country to country. They will also depend on different planned activities or accommodation whilst you're there. For example, you may need different vaccines if you're staying in a beach hut or safari camp compared to a hotel stay. Here are some of the more popular honeymoon destinations and the vaccines that are required before you travel.

◇ **Bali**: Tetanus, Hepatitis A, Typhoid and Poliomyelitis
◇ **Fiji**: Tetanus, Hepatitis A and Typhoid
◇ **Mauritius**: Tetanus, Hepatitis A and Typhoid
◇ **Maldives**: Tetanus, Hepatitis A and Typhoid
◇ **Jamaica**: Tetanus and Hepatitis A
◇ **South Africa**: Tetanus, Hepatitis A and Typhoid
◇ **Thailand**: Tetanus, Hepatitis A and Typhoid
◇ **Malaysia**: Tetanus, Hepatitis A and Typhoid
◇ **Cuba**: Tetanus, Hepatitis A and Typhoid

### When will I get treated?
If you're planning on going straight after your wedding, six to eight weeks before is ideal. It's sometimes possible to procure an emergency appointment the week of, or a few days before, your honeymoon.

### What happens afterwards?
Generally speaking, you should have no issues following your vaccines. If you do have any health related questions after your vaccinations, the majority of clinics will offer a 24/7 urgent cover service, which is helpful and reassuring.

# Popular Honeymoon Destinations For Irish Couples

## MALDIVES

**When to go:** December – February
**Don't miss:** Whale shark snorkeling and searching for turtles on the plentiful reefs.

Everywhere you look in the beautiful Maldives is like a postcard. Every picture looks photoshopped and when you get there you'll be taken aback that it could possibly be more stunning than you thought it would.

Each resort island has its own house reef for underwater exploring, while the seafood is unrivalled in its freshness. The locals are the friendliest people and couldn't be more willing to help and chat. You'll never want to leave this absolutely pristine island paradise.
*visitmaldives.com*

## THAILAND

**When to go:** November – February
**Don't miss:** A visit to an elephant sanctuary to bathe and feed the rescue elephants.

Boasting jungles, mountains, beaches, temples and palaces - Thailand is one of the friendliest places in the world, and is well known for being good value, so it's no surprise so many honeymooners flock there. Any of the tropical scenes the movie The Beach conjures up can be witnessed in real life (minus the weird beach cult, of course). After you've visited the temples, beaches and elephant sanctuary, a shopping trip around the floating Bangkok markets is a great way to round off your trip.
*tourismthailand.org*

## JAPAN

**When to go:** September – November
**Don't miss:** Take a Bullet train day trip to Lake Ashi and Mount Fuji and do some hiking.

Made up of thousands of unique islands, from tropical spots with crystal clear waters and white sandy beaches, to wildlife-rich locations and rain forests – there's a wealth of experiences to be had in Japan.

It's the ideal honeymoon destination to combine an island getaway with a city break; taking in some adventure, educational and historical experiences, and witnessing some of the most stunning scenery in the world. Unwind for a few days on one of the spectacular islands and then live it up in the bustling city of Tokyo - the best of both worlds.
*jnto.org.au*

## CUBA

**When to go:** December – March
**Don't miss:** See the beautiful pastel-coloured buildings in Havana and visit a cigar factory.

Whether you stay in a hotel or a casa particulares (private houses) you'll feel immediately immersed in the community of Cuban natives. In the capital, Havana, there's eye-popping views, cultural experiences aplenty and lots of lively nightlife. A trip to Varadero will reveal a laid-back beach atmosphere where you can laze on the sand or swim with dolphins. Cuba is the true gem of the Caribbean.
*cubatravel.cu/en*

## SOUTH AFRICA

**When to go:** May – August
**Don't miss:** A safari! See lions, leopards, rhinos and more in their natural habitat.

South Africa should feature on everyone's bucket list. It's got the perfect mix of adventure, sunshine, bustling cities and, of course, safaris. You can go cage diving with sharks off the southern coast of the Cape province, you can explore wineries in Paarl Valley and you can relax on the golden beaches at the southwest tip of the country. It's got a little bit of everything you fancy.
*southafrica.net*

## BALI

**When to go:** May – September
**Don't miss:** Visit Bali's iconic and beautiful temples; Tanah Lot, Uluwatu and Besakih.

Bali really has got it all. Both peaceful and serene for a couple of weeks of uninterrupted chill but with countless tours and excursions too. Day-tripping through Ubud and visiting temples will give you an idea of the rural side, while in Seminyak you can shop, eat and party in the more lively area of Bali.
*balitourismboard.org*

## GREECE

**When to go:** May – August
**Don't miss:** The sunsets. They are famous for being among the most picturesque in the world.

While Athens is steeped in history and culture, for honeymooners, island hopping is the dream. We recommend the Cyclades, which includes the islands of Mykonos, Santorini, Andros and Milos, where you can relax and party in equal measure.
*visitgreece.gr*

## NORTH AMERICA

**When to go:** Year round
**Don't miss:** The New Orleans Jazz & Heritage Festival is unmissable, as is a helicopter trip over the incredible Grand Canyon.

A huge country with so much to offer, it's hard to know which places to hit. Renting a car and driving Route 101 from LA to San Francisco is hard to top, followed by a couple of days in Las Vegas. New York is a must-see for anyone heading to the east coast and Boston's nearby. New Orleans is a special spot if you can squeeze it in!
*visittheusa.com*

# THINGS NO ONE TELLS YOU ABOUT YOUR HONEYMOON

After you get married, you have the rest of time with the love of your life to look forward to, but we'll bet the honeymoon is vying for first place on the list of things you're most excited about. However, while you might have planned for endless loved-up nights, perfect weather and complete bliss, there are a few things you might not expect...

### You can't switch relaxation on

Even couples that leave a gap between their wedding and honeymoon can find themselves totally zonked before boarding that plane. A blast of sunshine and a perfectly poured cocktail won't immediately bring you back to 100%, so allow a day or two to ease into holiday mode. Go with the flow, and maybe leave any big excursions for a couple of days, while you focus on chilling out together.

### You'll probably have nothing planned

For most holidays, you'll do research in advance on must-do/see things in your destination and where's best to eat and drink. That can all get lost in a haze of wedding planning, as all non-wedding related tasks tend to become future-you's problem. To make the most of your honeymoon, it's worth carving out a few hours to plan your trip so you don't arrive clueless and waste precious time.

### It might not be a 24/7 love-in

There may be petals on your bed every evening but that doesn't mean the whole trip is going to be rosy.

Even the fanciest lingerie won't win out against exhaustion at the end of a long day out and about – and that's okay. There's a certain romance in collapsing in a heap together, to eat room service and watch Netflix.

### Mishaps might happen

Whether it's that one, or both, of you is tetchy after flight delays, the hotel doesn't look exactly like it did in the pictures, or one of you ends up sick after eating some dodgy fish – these things can happen. Don't let it spoil your whole trip – roll with the punches and focus on spending quality time together.

### You'll come home feeling a whole lot closer

In your post-wedding, loved-up haze, you'll probably feel you've never be more in love but, your honeymoon will probably bring you even closer. Couples that share experiences and memories feel closer anyway, but it's a whole new level of excitement when you're celebrating and travelling for the first time as a married couple. You won't want to come home!

# Confetti loves...
## SELECTED SUPPLIERS

**MANDY WALSH - GOLD TRAVEL COUNSELLOR**
TEL: 046 948 3906
TRAVELCOUNSELLORS.IE/MANDY.WALSH

**SEYCHELLES TOURIST OFFICE**
TEL: 0207 730 0700
SEYCHELLES.TRAVEL

**SONHO A DOIS ALGARVE WEDDINGS**
TEL: +351 91 066 8928
SONHOADOIS.COM

# Honeymoon notes

# The Planner

## WHAT YOU'LL DO AND WHEN YOU'LL DO IT

# 12 Months Out

Week commencing ...............................................................................................................

...............................................................................................................

...............................................................................................................

...............................................................................................................

...............................................................................................................

...............................................................................................................

...............................................................................................................

...............................................................................................................

Week commencing ...............................................................................................................

...............................................................................................................

...............................................................................................................

...............................................................................................................

...............................................................................................................

...............................................................................................................

...............................................................................................................

...............................................................................................................

Week commencing .............................................................................................................

.............................................................................................................

.............................................................................................................

.............................................................................................................

.............................................................................................................

.............................................................................................................

.............................................................................................................

.............................................................................................................

Week commencing .............................................................................................................

.............................................................................................................

.............................................................................................................

.............................................................................................................

.............................................................................................................

.............................................................................................................

.............................................................................................................

.............................................................. Time to pick your venue!

# 11 Months Out

Week commencing .............................................................................

.........................................................................................................

.........................................................................................................

.........................................................................................................

.........................................................................................................

.........................................................................................................

.........................................................................................................

.........................................................................................................

Week commencing .............................................................................

.........................................................................................................

.........................................................................................................

.........................................................................................................

.........................................................................................................

.........................................................................................................

.........................................................................................................

........................................................... Have you booked your band?

.........................................................................................................

*Week commencing* ..................................................................................................

..................................................................................................

..................................................................................................

..................................................................................................

..................................................................................................

..................................................................................................

..................................................................................................

..................................................................................................

*Week commencing* ..................................................................................................

..................................................................................................

..................................................................................................

..................................................................................................

..................................................................................................

..................................................................................................

..................................................................................................

..................................................................................................

# 10 Months Out

Week commencing ...................................................................

...........................................................................................

...........................................................................................

...........................................................................................

...........................................................................................

...........................................................................................

...........................................................................................

Week commencing ...................................................................

...........................................................................................

...........................................................................................

...........................................................................................

...........................................................................................

...........................................................................................

...........................................................................................

...........................................................................................

Week commencing .........................................................................................................................................................

.................................................................................................................................................................................................

.................................................................................................................................................................................................

.................................................................................................................................................................................................

.................................................................................................................................................................................................

.................................................................................................................................................................................................

.................................................................................................................................................................................................

.................................................................................................................................................................................................

.................................................................. *Kick your skincare regime up a notch*

Week commencing .........................................................................................................................................................

.................................................................................................................................................................................................

.................................................................................................................................................................................................

.................................................................................................................................................................................................

.................................................................................................................................................................................................

.................................................................................................................................................................................................

.................................................................................................................................................................................................

.................................................................................................................................................................................................

# 9 Months Out

Week commencing .........................................................................................

.................................................................................................................

.................................................................................................................

.................................................................................................................

.................................................................................................................

.................................................................................................................

.................................................................................................................

.................................................................................... *Start dress shopping!*

Week commencing .........................................................................................

.................................................................................................................

.................................................................................................................

.................................................................................................................

.................................................................................................................

.................................................................................................................

.................................................................................................................

.................................................................................................................

Week commencing ........................................................................................................................

Week commencing ........................................................................................................................

# 8 Months Out

*Week commencing* ..........................................................................................

..........................................................................................

..........................................................................................

..........................................................................................

..........................................................................................

..........................................................................................

..........................................................................................

..........................................................................................

*Week commencing* ..........................................................................................

..........................................................................................

..........................................................................................

..........................................................................................

..........................................................................................

..........................................................................................

..........................................................................................

..........................................................................................

Week commencing ........................................................................................................................

........................................................................................................................

........................................................................................................................

........................................................................................................................

........................................................................................................................

........................................................................................................................

........................................................................................................................

........................................................................................................................

Week commencing ........................................................................................................................

........................................................................................................................

........................................................................................................................

........................................................................................................................

........................................................................................................................

........................................................................................................................

Book a fabulous florist ........................................................................................................................

........................................................................................................................

# 7 Months Out

Week commencing ............................................................................

....................................................................................................

....................................................................................................

....................................................................................................

....................................................................................................

....................................................................................................

....................................................................................................

....................................................................................................

Week commencing ............................................................................

....................................................................................................

....................................................................................................

....................................................................................................

....................................................................................................

....................................................................................................

....................................................................................................

Start thinking about your honeymoon ....................................................

*Week commencing* .........................................................................................

.........................................................................................................

.........................................................................................................

.........................................................................................................

.........................................................................................................

.........................................................................................................

.........................................................................................................

.........................................................................................................

*Week commencing* .........................................................................................

.........................................................................................................

.........................................................................................................

.........................................................................................................

.........................................................................................................

.........................................................................................................

.........................................................................................................

.........................................................................................................

# 6 Months Out

Week commencing ................................................................................................................

........................................................................................................................................

........................................................................................................................................

........................................................................................................................................

........................................................................................................................................

........................................................................................................................................

........................................................................................................................................

........................................................................................................................................

Week commencing ................................................................................................................

........................................................................................................................................

........................................................................................................................................

........................................................................................................................................

........................................................................................................................................

........................................................................................................................................

........................................................................................................................................

........................................................................................................................................

*Week commencing* ....................................................................................................

.................................................................................................................................

.................................................................................................................................

.................................................................................................................................

.................................................................................................................................

.................................................................................................................................

.................................................................................................................................

.................................................................................................................................

*Week commencing* ....................................................................................................

.................................................................................................................................

.................................................................................................................................

...................................................................................... *Send your Save The Dates*

.................................................................................................................................

.................................................................................................................................

.................................................................................................................................

.................................................................................................................................

# 5 Months Out

Week commencing .......................................................................................

.......................................................................................................................

.......................................................................................................................

.......................................................................................................................

.......................................................................................................................

Bridesmaids shopping time! .....................................................................

.......................................................................................................................

.......................................................................................................................

Week commencing .......................................................................................

.......................................................................................................................

.......................................................................................................................

.......................................................................................................................

.......................................................................................................................

.......................................................................................................................

.......................................................................................................................

.......................................................................................................................

.......................................................................................................................

*Week commencing* ....................................................................................................................

....................................................................................................................

....................................................................................................................

....................................................................................................................

....................................................................................................................

....................................................................................................................

....................................................................................................................

....................................................................................................................

....................................................................................................................

....................................................................................................................

*Week commencing* ....................................................................................................................

....................................................................................................................

....................................................................................................................

....................................................................................................................

....................................................................................................................

....................................................................................................................

....................................................................................................................

....................................................................................................................

....................................................................................................................

....................................................................................................................

# 4 Months Out

Week commencing ...........................................................................................

.................................................................................................................

.................................................................................................................

.................................................................................................................

.................................................................................................................

.................................................................................................................

.................................................................................................................

.................................................................................................................

Week commencing ...........................................................................................

.................................................................................................................

.................................................................................................................

.................................................................................................................

.................................................................................................................

.................................................................................................................

.................................................................................................................

.................................................................................................................

Week commencing ...........................................................................................................

............................................................................................................................

............................................................................................................................

............................................................................................................................

............................................................................................................................

............................................................................................................................

............................................................................................................................

............................................................................................................................

Week commencing ...........................................................................................................

............................................................................................................................

............................................................................................................................

............................................................................................................................

............................................................................................................................

............................................................................................................................

..................................................... Have you got your legalities sorted?

............................................................................................................................

# 3 Months Out

Week commencing ........................................................................................

........................................................................................

........................................................................................

........................................................................................

........................................................................................

........................................................................................

........................................................................................

........................................................................................

........................................................................................

Week commencing ........................................................................................

........................................................................................

........................................................................................

........................................................................................

........................................................................................

........................................................................................

........................................................ *Having a gift list? Time to write it!*

........................................................................................

*Week commencing* ......................................................................................................................

..................................................................................................................................................

..................................................................................................................................................

..................................................................................................................................................

..................................................................................................................................................

..................................................................................................................................................

..................................................................................................................................................

*Week commencing* ......................................................................................................................

..................................................................................................................................................

..................................................................................................................................................

..................................................................................................................................................

..................................................................................................................................................

..................................................................................................................................................

..................................................................................................................................................

# 2 Months Out

Week commencing .............................................................................................

.............................................................................................

.............................................................................................

.............................................................................................

.............................................................................................

.............................................................................................

.............................................................................................

.............................................................................................

Week commencing .............................................................................................

.............................................................................................

.............................................................................................

.............................................................................................

.............................................................................................

.............................................................................................

.............................................................................................

.............................................................................................

.............................................................................................

Week commencing ...........................................................................................................................................

...........................................................................................................................................

...........................................................................................................................................

...........................................................................................................................................

...........................................................................................................................................

...........................................................................................................................................

...........................................................................................................................................

...........................................................................................................................................

Week commencing ...........................................................................................................................................

...........................................................................................................................................

...........................................................................................................................................

...........................................................................................................................................

..................................................................................................................... *Send your invitations!*

...........................................................................................................................................

...........................................................................................................................................

...........................................................................................................................................

# 1 Month Out

Week commencing .................................................................................................................

.................................................................................................................................................

.................................................................................................................................................

.................................................................................................................................................

.................................................................................................................................................

.................................................................................................................................................

.................................................................................................................................................

.................................................................................................................................................

.................................................................................................................................................

Week commencing .................................................................................................................

.................................................................................................................................................

.................................................................................................................................................

.................................................................................................................................................

.................................................................................................................................................

.................................................................................................................................................

You're getting married, this month! ...............................................................................

.................................................................................................................................................

.................................................................................................................................................

*Week commencing* .............................................................................................

.............................................................................................

.............................................................................................

.............................................................................................

.............................................................................................

.............................................................................................

.............................................................................................

.............................................................................................

*Week commencing* .............................................................................................

.............................................................................................

.............................................................................................

.............................................................................................

.............................................................................................

.............................................................................................

.............................................................................................

.............................................................................................

# YOU'RE THE MEASURE OF my dreams, THE MEASURE OF MY DREAMS

The Pogues

# Day-Of Timeline

7am .......................................................................................................................

8am .......................................................................................................................

9am .......................................................................................................................

10am .....................................................................................................................

11am .....................................................................................................................

12pm .....................................................................................................................

1pm .......................................................................................................................

2pm .......................................................................................................................

3pm .......................................................................................................................

4pm .......................................................................................................................

5pm .......................................................................................................................

6pm .......................................................................................................................

7pm .......................................................................................................................

8pm .......................................................................................................................

9pm .......................................................................................................................

10pm .....................................................................................................................

11pm .....................................................................................................................

12am .....................................................................................................................

# Emergency Kit Checklist

| | | | |
|---|---|---|---|
| Lipstick | ☐ | Hair clips | ☐ |
| Lip balm | ☐ | Heel protectors | ☐ |
| Powder/blotting sheets | ☐ | Gel insoles | ☐ |
| Comb | ☐ | Plasters | ☐ |
| Tissues | ☐ | Nail file | ☐ |
| Wet wipes | ☐ | Nail polish | ☐ |
| Cotton buds | ☐ | Mints/gum | ☐ |
| Deodorant | ☐ | Painkillers | ☐ |
| Fragrance | ☐ | Phone charger | ☐ |
| Safety pins | ☐ | Compact mirror | ☐ |

# Emergency Contact List

Best Man .................................................................................................................

Maid of honour .......................................................................................................

Venue contact .........................................................................................................

Church contact (if applicable) ...............................................................................

Wedding planner ....................................................................................................

Wedding stylist/décor hire ....................................................................................

Celebrant ................................................................................................................

Caterer ...................................................................................................................

Photographer .........................................................................................................

Videographer .........................................................................................................

Florist .....................................................................................................................

Cake supplier .........................................................................................................

Band contact ..........................................................................................................

DJ contact ..............................................................................................................

Ceremony musicians .............................................................................................

Transport company ...............................................................................................

Entertainment contact ..........................................................................................

Day two food suppliers .........................................................................................

Day two entertainment .........................................................................................

# Morning Jobs to Delegate

On your wedding day, your only job is to relax and enjoy it. Delegate all jobs to a responsible person and try to forget about it – your work here is done.

### Taking calls from suppliers
Give your maid of honour or best man's mobile numbers to all suppliers as their day-of contact. If they're having trouble finding the venue, or they're not sure where to place the wedding cake, someone else can take care of it.

### Payments
Hand over all pre-prepared vendor payments to a person from the wedding party – traditionally, the best man.

### Collecting gifts
Similarly, assign someone to take care of any pressies or cards you receive from generous guests.

### Micro-logistics
Who will carry your bridal emergency kit? Or mind your phone until after the ceremony? Bridesmaids probably need their hands free for walking up the aisle, so assign a trusted friend to carry your bits and get them to you safely, when you're settled.

### Décor recce
If you've given some styling elements to your venue to display, or you don't get a window to check out the florist's handiwork before the ceremony, you're forgiven for feeling anxious in case everything isn't where you'd like it. Why not ask someone to do a recce, take some pics and send them to you for your seal of approval? Then you can relax knowing everything's as it should be.

*"Why not ask someone to do a recce, take some pics and send them to you for your seal of approval?"*

# VENDOR PAYMENTS TO HAVE PREPARED

Some suppliers will request payment in advance, but for those who require cash payments on the day, here's a handy checklist.

- Any remaining venue payments ☐
- Celebrant ☐
- Photographer ☐
- Videographer ☐
- Hair stylist ☐
- Makeup artist ☐
- Florist ☐
- Caterer ☐
- Cake supplier ☐
- Band ☐
- DJ ☐
- Ceremony musicians ☐
- Transport ☐
- Other entertainment ☐
- Photobooth ☐
- Day two entertainers ☐

# Gifts To Give

Don't forget to arrange little tokens
of appreciation for these people

Something meaningful for each other .......................................... ☐

Bridesmaids and groomsmen ..................................................... ☐

Flower girls and page boys ........................................................ ☐

Your parents ................................................................................. ☐

Close friends and wedding helpers .......................................... ☐

If you're including the old school ritual of bouquets for
mammies during the speeches, don't forget
to order them in advance ............................................................ ☐

# DON'T FORGET TO THANK

Writing a speech? Don't leave these important
people out of your thank yous

◇ Your new husband or wife

◇ Both sets of parents

◇ Step-parents, if applicable

◇ The best man/woman and maid/man of honour

◇ The rest of your wedding party

◇ Flower girls and page boys

◇ Non wedding party friends who helped out

◇ The staff at your venue

◇ Your celebrant, priest or minister

◇ Those who made your hen or stag party special

◇ Anyone who contributed financially, or with their time

◇ Anyone involved on the day (singers, readers etc.)

◇ The person who introduced you to each other, if applicable.

# What To Pack
## for your wedding

### Fashion bits
◇ Wedding dress
◇ Veil and headpiece
◇ Wedding outerwear
◇ Pretty hanger to display it all
◇ Shapewear or lingerie
◇ Wedding shoes (including a change/flats for later)
◇ Wedding bag
◇ Jewellery and accessories
◇ Suit, waistcoat and shirt
◇ Tie/bowtie and pocket square
◇ Cufflinks, braces and socks
◇ Wedding morning robe or pretty pyjamas and slippers
◇ Rehearsal dinner outfit, shoes and accessories
◇ Second day outfit, shoes and accessories

### Practicalities
◇ Sunglasses and SPF
◇ Umbrella
◇ Painkillers, allergy tablets and any other medication
◇ Emergency kit (see page 264)
◇ Bluetooth speaker for wedding morning tunes
◇ Phone charger and a fully charged battery pack

### Beauty
◇ Makeup for touch-ups
◇ Wedding fragrances
◇ General toiletries
◇ Skincare
◇ Wedding morning scented candle

### Admin
◇ Cash payments for suppliers
◇ Emergency contact list (see page 265 for who to include)
◇ Paperwork for the ceremony

### Don't forget
◇ Wedding rings
◇ Vows
◇ Speeches
◇ Your something borrowed, something blue etc.
◇ Sentimental items
◇ A piece of your wedding stationery, to be photographed
◇ Wedding party gifts

# My Packing List

# IF YOU'VE DECIDED TO CHANGE YOUR NAME...

Once you've obtained your wedding certificate,
you can start the process of changing your name.
Here's our handy list of things to check off.

Passport ............................................................................................ ☐

Driver licence ................................................................................... ☐

Details on the live register (voting) ....................................... ☐

Bank accounts and cards ............................................................ ☐

Car registration and insurance .............................................. ☐

Phone bill and any utility bills in your name/s ............... ☐

# Wedding Gifts Log

It's a good idea to keep a record of gifts received from your guests, so you can thank them properly afterwards. Make a note here to jog your memory when you're writing your thank you cards.

| Guest | Gift received |
|-------|---------------|
| Guest ............................................ | Gift received ........................................ |
| Guest ............................................ | Gift received ........................................ |
| Guest ............................................ | Gift received ........................................ |
| Guest ............................................ | Gift received ........................................ |
| Guest ............................................ | Gift received ........................................ |
| Guest ............................................ | Gift received ........................................ |
| Guest ............................................ | Gift received ........................................ |
| Guest ............................................ | Gift received ........................................ |
| Guest ............................................ | Gift received ........................................ |
| Guest ............................................ | Gift received ........................................ |
| Guest ............................................ | Gift received ........................................ |
| Guest ............................................ | Gift received ........................................ |
| Guest ............................................ | Gift received ........................................ |
| Guest ............................................ | Gift received ........................................ |
| Guest ............................................ | Gift received ........................................ |
| Guest ............................................ | Gift received ........................................ |
| Guest ............................................ | Gift received ........................................ |
| Guest ............................................ | Gift received ........................................ |

# Wedding Gifts Log

| | |
|---|---|
| Guest ........................................ | Gift received ........................................ |
| Guest ........................................ | Gift received ........................................ |
| Guest ........................................ | Gift received ........................................ |
| Guest ........................................ | Gift received ........................................ |
| Guest ........................................ | Gift received ........................................ |
| Guest ........................................ | Gift received ........................................ |
| Guest ........................................ | Gift received ........................................ |
| Guest ........................................ | Gift received ........................................ |
| Guest ........................................ | Gift received ........................................ |
| Guest ........................................ | Gift received ........................................ |
| Guest ........................................ | Gift received ........................................ |
| Guest ........................................ | Gift received ........................................ |
| Guest ........................................ | Gift received ........................................ |
| Guest ........................................ | Gift received ........................................ |
| Guest ........................................ | Gift received ........................................ |
| Guest ........................................ | Gift received ........................................ |
| Guest ........................................ | Gift received ........................................ |
| Guest ........................................ | Gift received ........................................ |
| Guest ........................................ | Gift received ........................................ |
| Guest ........................................ | Gift received ........................................ |
| Guest ........................................ | Gift received ........................................ |

Guest ...............................................    Gift received .............................................

Guest ...............................................    Gift received .............................................

Guest ...............................................    Gift received .............................................

Guest ...............................................    Gift received .............................................

Guest ...............................................    Gift received .............................................

Guest ...............................................    Gift received .............................................

Guest ...............................................    Gift received .............................................

Guest ...............................................    Gift received .............................................

Guest ...............................................    Gift received .............................................

Guest ...............................................    Gift received .............................................

Guest ...............................................    Gift received .............................................

Guest ...............................................    Gift received .............................................

Guest ...............................................    Gift received .............................................

Guest ...............................................    Gift received .............................................

Guest ...............................................    Gift received .............................................

Guest ...............................................    Gift received .............................................

Guest ...............................................    Gift received .............................................

Guest ...............................................    Gift received .............................................

Guest ...............................................    Gift received .............................................

Guest ...............................................    Gift received .............................................

# Wedding Gifts Log

Guest ........................................................ Gift received ........................................................

Guest ........................................................ Gift received ........................................................

Guest ........................................................ Gift received ........................................................

Guest ........................................................ Gift received ........................................................

Guest ........................................................ Gift received ........................................................

Guest ........................................................ Gift received ........................................................

Guest ........................................................ Gift received ........................................................

Guest ........................................................ Gift received ........................................................

Guest ........................................................ Gift received ........................................................

Guest ........................................................ Gift received ........................................................

Guest ........................................................ Gift received ........................................................

Guest ........................................................ Gift received ........................................................

Guest ........................................................ Gift received ........................................................

Guest ........................................................ Gift received ........................................................

Guest ........................................................ Gift received ........................................................

Guest ........................................................ Gift received ........................................................

Guest ........................................................ Gift received ........................................................

Guest ........................................................ Gift received ........................................................

Guest ........................................................ Gift received ........................................................

Guest ........................................................ Gift received ........................................................

| Guest | Gift received |
|-------|---------------|
| Guest | Gift received |
| Guest | Gift received |
| Guest | Gift received |
| Guest | Gift received |
| Guest | Gift received |
| Guest | Gift received |
| Guest | Gift received |
| Guest | Gift received |
| Guest | Gift received |
| Guest | Gift received |
| Guest | Gift received |
| Guest | Gift received |
| Guest | Gift received |
| Guest | Gift received |
| Guest | Gift received |
| Guest | Gift received |
| Guest | Gift received |
| Guest | Gift received |
| Guest | Gift received |
| Guest | Gift received |

# A Word From The Author

can hardly believe this is *The Wedding Planner*'s third edition. Weddings are constantly evolving, and each new issue of *Confetti* offers up the latest trends, the season's most beautiful real weddings and up-to-date décor inspiration – all with our distinctly Irish style and *Confetti* twist. But we also wanted to create something for the newly engaged couple, starting from scratch; a planning oracle where no question goes unanswered and an all-encompassing, no nonsense, bridal bible. An idea became a dream and, before we knew it, the little book that could was out there in the wild. The response was instantaneous and overwhelming, with a copy selling every ten minutes across the country. And here we are, three years later, with an updated edition for 2020.

*The Wedding Planner* is a huge team effort and I'm so incredibly proud to be part of Team *Confetti*. It's no mean feat to make a niche publication like ours a household name, but we've done just that. And our bragging rights were solidified when we recently became Irish Magazine of the Year for the second year in a row (we're still recovering from the celebrations). We're also the only Irish wedding magazine with a premium digital offering, and it's safe to say we have social sewn up. In everything we do, we try to elevate our offering above the standard, the finest example of which is the recent introduction of *Confetti Live*. Part live show, part wedding expo, part brilliant, bridal day out – it's like nothing else out there. In short, we don't do things by half.

Of course, without the unending loyalty of our *Confetti* readers, none of this would be our reality. You're the greatest bunch of lads. Thank you so much for continuing to support all that we do.

Mam, this one (and everything else) is for you.

*Laura Cunningham*

WHO SAYS I SHOULD LET
*a wild one*
GO FREE?

Boy Meets Girl